WITHDRAWN
HARVARD LIBRARY
WITHDRAWN

Writers of Wales

EDITORS

MEIC STEPHENS   R. BRINLEY JONES

The Nine *Juvencus* englynion

D. Simon Evans

MEDIEVAL
RELIGIOUS
LITERATURE

*University of Wales Press
on behalf of the Welsh Arts Council*

1986

PB
2207
E92
1986

I

nit guorgnim molim mab meir
(it is not too much toil to praise the Son of Mary)

This is a line out of the earliest bits of Welsh preserved on vellum, the first indication of what was later to become the prevailing, indeed unflagging, attitude of the Welshman down until recent times. Never did he regard it as irksome to praise God; his main concern was to find ways and means of adequately expressing his thoughts and feelings about a God who gave and did so much.

This line, and the nine religious stanzas where it occurs, is to be found on an empty space in a Latin manuscript containing a metrical version of the Gospels. They were written in by a nameless cleric sometime between the ninth and eleventh centuries, at a time when it was not considered necessary or appropriate for a whole page of precious vellum to be expended on Welsh. Written Welsh, however, was now resolutely edging in, and before long it was to be accorded fuller and more honourable space.

In the Wales of those times there were two distinguishable cultures. The one was native, and used the vernacular. The other was 'foreign', and used a foreign language, namely Latin, the language of a vanished empire, whose imprint was, however, still to be seen and felt. Then there was the new Christian faith, which had both supplanted and in part helped to sustain the influence of the earlier empire. Of these two cultures, one was in origin oral, the other written. For the first, we may in the main refer to the poets in Wales, corresponding broadly to the *filid* in Ireland. They were involved not only with poetry, as we know it, but also with traditional lore, history, law, genealogy, and were disposed to uphold and promote values usually described as 'heroic'. That everybody did not subscribe to such values, however, is evident from the attitude of the sixth-century author Gildas, who denounces Maelgwn, prince of Gwynedd, for giving ear to praises sung to him by the poets rather than to praises sung to God. And it must be conceded that in the works of sixth- and seventh-century poets, like Taliesin and Aneirin, there is little (if any) real evidence of concern for Christian values. We find little evidence also in some later (and different) poetry, notably the ninth-century *englynion* from Powys associated with the names of Llywarch Hen and Heledd.

The tenth-century poem ARMES PRYDEIN (*c*.930) is different, in its provenance and purpose. It can hardly have been composed by a poet of the traditional order, but rather by an ecclesiastic (probably associated with the cult of Saint David), whose aim was not to magnify a prince, so much as to secure stability and dignity for the Welsh in their confrontation with the Anglo-Saxon intruders. During the early centuries, from the sixth through to the eleventh, we are able to observe, albeit sporadically, the progressively prominent role of the ecclesiastic in the literary as well as in the religious and political life of Wales. After all, it was he alone who had any pretensions to learning and literacy. Ecclesiastics only (some of them, but not all) knew Latin, the one written medium, and there is evidence that texts on varied subjects in that language were studied in earnest by Welshmen, more especially during the ninth and tenth centuries. Some of the notes and comments made by these dedicated students, in the margins or between the lines of the Latin text—the so-called glosses—still survive. The Welsh now found it necessary to explain to themselves (and to others) the Latin they were studying, a language which they obviously knew only imperfectly. Evidence of this is forthcoming from other sources. We need only compare the Latin of Gildas in the sixth century with that of 'Nennius' at the beginning of the ninth to realize how far competence in the language had deteriorated.

However, along with this decline in the knowledge of Latin, as we approach the Norman period, we are able to discern a development which was to have the effect eventually of blurring the distinction between the two cultures already mentioned. The new virile medium Welsh, which had developed some centuries earlier from the parent British, now became a language not only to be spoken and heard, but also to be written and read. Some nameless scholar or scholars had devised for it an orthography based on that of Latin, and as we have already seen, in the early period attempts were made to write it.

The contribution of those ecclesiastics who first committed Welsh to writing has not to date been duly recognized. In many ways, they could be regarded as 'authors', in that for the first time they produced in written form prose and poetry which had hitherto only been spoken. Their work, and the progress generally made in this new exercise, must have formed part of a renaissance, a Welsh renaissance which may be dated to some time between the eighth and eleventh centuries, and associated with the reigns of kings like Rhodri Mawr in the ninth century, and Hywel Dda in the tenth.

The pieces of Welsh found in the pre-Norman period, before the twelfth century, contain very little literature. There is some poetry; three short poems in all, none of which is in the tradition of earlier heroic verse. One consists of three stanzas, evidently from a cycle akin to that of the Llywarch Hen and Heledd poems. In the same manuscript occur the nine religious stanzas referred to above (a metrical adaptation of a scriptural text), while a solitary stanza to Cyrwen, the staff of St Padarn, is found in a late eleventh-century manuscript, which contains a copy of Augustine's DE TRINITATE made by Ieuan, one of the sons of Sulien of Llanbadarn, of whom more will be said later.

The nine stanzas were composed in praise of the Trinity, and as occasionally in the case of later religious verse, they are 'stiffened' with some Latin; *Omnipotens Auctor (Almighty Lord)* are the opening words. In the line quoted above the author exults in the opportunity offered to praise Jesus, the son of Mary *(map Meir)*. It is not too much toil or labour; *nit guor gnim* are his words. Here we find a new medium expressing new hope and vigour, a new faith and vision, which is in sharp contrast to the use of *gnim (toil, labour)* in a famous stanza from Llywarch Hen, where the poet thinks of his life as being dominated by a stern, unyielding fate *(tynget)* ever since he was born—at night! The toil is long and weary, with no relief:

> *Truan a dynget a dynget y Lywarch*
> *Er y nos y ganet:*
> *Hir gnim heb escor lludet.*

> *(Sorry is the fate allotted to Llywarch*
> *Since the night he was born:*
> *Long toil, with no relief from fatigue.)*

So much then for the old period, which can only offer scraps of Welsh in Latin manuscripts. With the twelfth century we enter a new phase in the history of life and culture in Wales, as elsewhere. From then on there is no lack of written material, and over the next four centuries or so we find an abundance of manuscripts (approximately a hundred in all) devoted mainly or exclusively to Welsh. These contain different kinds of literature, among which religion looms large. For collections containing religious verse we may mention the following: THE BLACK BOOK OF CARMARTHEN, the earliest complete Welsh manuscript (twelfth/thirteenth century), THE BOOK OF TALIESIN (c.1325), THE RED BOOK OF HERGEST (c. 1375–1425), and LLAWYSGRIF HENDREGADREDD (c. 1300).

Let us look at the poetry in these, and other manuscripts. First, the earlier Gogynfeirdd, or, as they are also called, the Poets of the Princes, who belong in the main to the twelfth and thirteenth centuries, the final period of Welsh political independence. Most of them belonged to Gwynedd in the north-west. They sang to the princes Gruffudd ap Cynan (d.1137), Llywelyn ab Iorwerth (d.1240), Llywelyn ap Gruffudd (d. 1282), and others, and in eulogy and elegy extolled those heroic and other qualities characteristic of the model leader. But they were also respectful of Christian values, and in their work and outlook represent a blend of the two cultures which at an earlier period seemed to have remained separate, a blend produced by the medieval mind in which the imprimatur of the Church is all-pervading.

Such blending seems reflected in the adaptation in a religious context of terms hitherto exclusively employed for secular poetry. These are native words, unlike the bulk of Christian vocabulary in Welsh which, as in other languages, is derived from Latin. Here are some random examples, taken from *HGCr: kerennyd (friendship)* 59.42, *kyuarws (boon)* 25.62, *kymodi (to be reconciled)* 76.26, *dadolwch (reconciliation)* 65.13, *direid (evil)* 20.19, *diwyccom-ne (let us make amends)* 4.1, *gwledic (lord, chief)*

11.9, 13.68, *gwrda (lord, nobleman)* 21.5, *llyw (leader)* 29.81, *mechdeyrn (king)* 62.12, 64.84, *neb kystal (no one like/equal)* 11.6, *peir (lord, chieftain)* 27.15, *recouyt (dispenser of gifts)* 29.42, 27.34, 65.8, *ri (king)* 29.83, 72.22, *tanc (peace)* 57.135.

The religious poetry of the Gogynfeirdd was edited many years ago (in 1931) by the late Professor Henry Lewis in a volume entitled HEN GERDDI CREFYDDOL. Reference has already been made to the involvement of the Welsh with religion over the centuries. Changes and innovations are witnessed at various stages, but these are mostly attributable to influences or pressures from without, or to special conditions and circumstances from within. The beliefs and practices, and, generally the thoughts, concepts and images of the Welsh are mostly such as are found elsewhere also at this time and later.

Let us now note briefly certain features of interest in the earlier poetry. As one would expect, there is emphasis on the frailty of human life, and on the uncertainty and insecurity of wealth and power:

> *Ny cheiff kyuoethawc uot yn hirhoedlawc*
>
> (*The wealthy/powerful will not be allowed long life.*)
> (HEN GERDDI CREFYDDOL, 79.33)

There is emphasis on the transitoriness of the world:

> *Pop pressent ys hawod*

(Every worldly thing is of summer's duration.)
(ibid., 20(xii) 6)

This was stressed by the monasteries, and consequent upon their progress in the twelfth century there was experienced in the Church a revival of piety, with the accent on inner experience.

We may refer to some more specific concepts and beliefs, characteristic of the medieval mind, which thought of the universe as ordered and carefully graded, with its structure conceived of as a great chain or ladder of degrees of being, extending from the very throne of God through all possible grades down to the most meagre of objects. There was ultimate unity in the universe which was solidly theocentric.

One is struck by the significance of numbers, specific and specified. The poets knew of the *four* elements *(y pedwar defnydd)*: fire, water, air, earth. The great Cynddelw (c.1155–1200) speaks of God as having formed him from them:

> *A'm peris o'r pedwar defnyt*
>
> *(Who formed me from the four elements.)*
(ibid., 39.208)

We also find mention of *seven*—mist, flowers and mind, in addition to the four:

> *O seith lauanad ban im se suinad*
>
> *(From seven elements was I formed.)*
(ibid., 7.50)

There were *nine* (angelic) orders of heaven *(naw rad nef)*, who gave protection and blessing (ibid. 9.19, 85.41). Casnodyn (c.1320–40) and others speak of *ten* orders, and also of *twelve* (THE MYVYRIAN ARCHAIOLOGY OF WALES, 285 b 2,22). Although angels were not favoured by the Early Church, their position later improved, especially after Constantine became a Christian. Their veneration was authorized by the Seventh Council in 787, and individuals among them, such as Michael and Gabriel, were commonly referred to and their help invoked. Michael was recognized as fighter, champion and rescuer, while Gabriel was revered as God's messenger; he was the herald of the Incarnation.

The *five* ages of the world *(pumoes byd)* are often mentioned, to denote the 'lost' ages before the coming of the Deliverer. These extended from the Creation to Noah, from Noah to Abraham, from Abraham to Moses, from Moses to David, and from David to Christ, who through His suffering delivered all five from the bondage of hell:

'
> Can duc pymwan Crist pym oes a gaeth
>
> (*Since the five wounds of Christ brought five ages from bondage.*)
>
> (HEN GERDDI . . ., 56.109)
>
> A warawd pym oes byd o geithiwed uffern
>
> (*Who rescued the five ages of the world from the bondage of hell.*)
>
> (ibid., 83.73)

Chwech oes byd (the six ages of the world), mentioned by Einion ap Gwalchmai c.1203–23 (ibid. 66.48), would seem to cover all the ages, including the one after Christ, although other divisions and calculations are also possible!

Seven was, of course, a number often specified. The Gogynfeirdd and later poets knew of the *seven* deadly sins *(seith briwyt pechawt)*:

> *Seith briwyt pechawt yw pechodeu yr bobyl,*
> *Mae yn y Bibyl eu henweu*
>
> *(The seven deadly sins are the sins of the people,*
> *Their names are in the Bible)*
> (ibid., 99.23–24)

In *R* 1238–9 they are enumerated as follows: *syberwyt (pride), kynghoruynt (envy), llit (wrath), llesged (indolence), kebydyaeth (meanness), glythineb (gluttony), godineb (adultery)*. There are, however, other lists of seven, with slight variations. Among the earlier Gogynfeirdd there is also occasionally reference to *eight* such sins (e.g. *HGCr* 24.46), a number doubtless ultimately derived from Cassian, the famous eastern monk and writer of the early fifth century; but they are not enumerated. It is said, however, that of the eight *syberwyt* is the worst:

> *O'r wyth gwyth gwaethaf syberwyt*
>
> *(Of the eight deadly sins the worst is pride.)*
> (ibid., 78.35)

In order to heal men's souls of such sins, God gave the seven deeds of mercy. They consisted of feeding the hungry, giving drink to the thirsty and clothes to the naked, harbouring the wayfaring, attending to the sick, freeing the prisoner, and burying the dead. Questions would be asked at the Last Judgement as to how these duties had been discharged, and Christ would remind people how He had appeared on earth in the guise of the weak, the needy, and the wounded. For those unable to give such practical help, other more spiritual works were urged, such as the comforting of the sad and bereaved. Opposed to the seven sins were the *seven* virtues: *ufuddawt (humility), haelyoni (generosity), karyat (love), diweirdeb (chastity), kymedrolder (moderation), anmyned (patience), ehutrwyd (eagerness)* (cf. THE ELUCIDARIUM AND OTHER TEXTS, 145–6).

The reference above to the Bible is of interest, since it raises the important question of the extent to which these poets were familiar with its contents, which were for the most part in Latin. There is evidence that knowledge of the scriptures among the poets improved during our period. Biblical characters are mentioned, such as Adam, Eve, Cain, Abel, Enoch, Abraham, Absalom, Judas, Herod and Pilate, the Four Evangelists and Paul. It is clear that some historical sections of both the Old and New Testaments were known. Cynddelw, for example, knew of the apple tasted by Eve (HEN GERDDI ..., 29.99), and the story and circumstances attending the birth of Jesus were familiar. It is recounted in detail by the friar Madog ap Gwallter (*c.*1250) in a delightful poem (ibid. 105–7), which has been described as the oldest Christmas carol in Welsh. Here are some lines:

Great giant small and frail,
So mighty yet so weak, with cheek how pale,
So rich, so poor is he,
Our Father-Brother and our Judge to be ...
So high, so low reclined,
Emmanuel, honeyed thoughts make sweet his mind ...
Not in rich satin dight,
His rags now unlike amianthus white,
Nor yet in sendal laid,
But poorest tatters furnish forth his bed ...
What herald doth he send
To shepherds who their folded flocks do tend?
It is an angel bright,
And straightway clear as noonday grows the night ...
Lo, Christmas night is here,
Night fairer far than earth's of doubt and fear,
When Christian folk will sing
For joy of heart; joy's offering let us bring.
(Trans. A HISTORY OF WELSH LITERATURE, 56–57)

However, acquaintance with large sections of the accepted canon is not evidenced in the poetry of the Gogynfeirdd. What we do find in their works is the traditional teaching of the Church, its liturgy and its preaching, and in some cases its pictures and images. They also inherited certain features from their predecessors, the Cynfeirdd. One such was the latter's predilection for praise, praise for princes, but in their case for God also, and His saints. According to the Welsh laws, it was the duty of the *pencerdd* or chief poet at court at the king's request to sing two songs, one of God and the other of the kings, a dual assignment, indicative of a custom which may be traced to an early stage in the history of Indo-European culture, as Professor Caerwyn Williams has suggested. In many respects the poet must have regarded his relationship to God as not essentially different from his relationship to his patron, the prince.

The Bardic Grammars, the earliest known copies of which date from c.1350–1400, laid down guidelines on how to praise all kinds of persons, God, Mary, saints, prelates and others. Here the imprimatur of the Church is quite evident, for the poets must have been affected by its influence for quite some time. As an example of an effusion of praise to God we may take a poem in the BLACK BOOK OF CARMARTHEN in which He is addressed thus:

> *Gogonedauc Argluit, hanpich guell;*
> *A'th uendicco -de egluis a chagell,*
> *A'th uendicco -de kagell ac egluis,*
> *A'th uendicco -de vastad a diffuis*
>
> *(Glorious Lord, hail!*
> *May church and chancel,*
> *May chancel and church,*
> *May plain and abyss, glorify thee.)*
>   (ibid., 1.1–4)

Another is an ode by Meilyr ap Gwalchmai (c. 1170–1220), which begins with the words,

> *Duw Arglwyd, erglyw dy volyant*
>
> *(Lord God, hear thy praise.)*
>   (ibid., 60.1)

God is described as being without peer, a description often given of the chieftain in the early poetry:

> *Ny dhoeth ny dhyfydh neb cystal a Dovydh,*
> *Ny aned mewn plwyw neb cystal a Dyw*
>
> (*There came not, there comes not anyone equal to the Lord,*
> *There was not born in a parish anyone equal to God.*)
> (ibid., 14.6–7)

He is eternal, transcending time:

> *Diwet ny byt yt, na dechreu ny bu*
>
> (*There will be no end to Thee, neither was there a beginning.*)
> (ibid., 66.29)

He is, of course, the one supreme ruler:

> *Vch nef is nef nyt gwledic namyn ef*
>
> (*Above heaven, below heaven, He only is ruler.*)
> (ibid., 11.9)

and described as

> *naf a llyw pob kyueir*
>
> (*lord and leader of every part.*)
> (THE POETRY IN THE RED BOOK OF HERGEST, 1330.24)

It was He who created us:

> *Vch mor is mor ef a'n crewys*
>
> (*Above the sea, below the sea, it was He who created us.*)
>
> (HEN GERDDI..., 11.10)

People believe in Him:

> *Y'r Creawdyr a'e crewys y credant*
>
> (*In the Creator who created them they believe.*)
>
> (ibid., 61.16)

Belief is again stressed by Meilyr ap Gwalchmai (c.1170–1220):

> *Credu y Duw a'e dawn ys kyfyawnhaf*
>
> (*It is most right to believe in God and His bounty.*)
>
> (ibid., 60.34)

Of poets from the Gogynfeirdd (early and late), who composed poems to God, we may cite also Gwalchmai ap Meilyr (c.1130–80), Cynddelw (c.1155–1200), Llywarch Brydydd y Moch (c. 1173–1220), Einion ap Gwalchmai (c.1203–23), Madog ap Gwallter (c. 1250), Gruffudd ap Maredudd (c.1350–90) and others.

We have already noted a very early poem in praise of the Trinity. Such devotion continued among the poets throughout the medieval period. It is expressed in a poem in the BLACK BOOK OF CARMARTHEN, and in a masterly sequence of awdlau by the fourteenth-century poet Casnodyn, who represents the religious poetry of the late Gogynfeirdd at its best. Dafydd ap Gwilym asserts that heaven and earth were made for us by the Trinity. They are devoutly praised by Gruffudd Llwyd (c.1380–1420), as austerity tightens its grip on him in his later years, and praise for them is the theme of three out of eighteen poems by Ieuan Brydydd Hir (c.1450). Lewis Glyn Cothi's longest awdl is devoted to them.

During this period the cult of Mary progressed further, as she became the object of deep affection and reverence, fostered by the Cistercians and later by the friars. The poets found much pleasure in describing her qualities and her varying relationships as a member of the Heavenly Family:

> *She is mother to her father, she is undeniably a virgin,*
> *She is a dispenser of gifts, wholly generous,*
> *She is thus a daughter to her son the way it is,*
> *She is sister to God of godly faith.*
> (Trans. ibid., 24.21–4)

She is the one to whom the sinner offers supplication (ibid. 83.87), and Meilyr ap Gwalchmai (c. 1170–1220) wants her to intercede for him with her son—*mabkwas* (ibid. 64.97). She is described as the 'sinless virgin' *(morwyn dibech,* THE POETRY IN THE RED BOOK OF HERGEST, 1248.8); unlike all other humans, she had been born without sin, a doctrine advanced by Duns Scotus in the fourteenth century and popularized by the Franciscans.

Apocryphal stories relating to Jesus, His mother and His father Joseph, are told in some poems, notably the account of the flight to Egypt, a widely popular tale which also proved attractive to artists. The Welsh version in the Black Book of Carmarthen is the earliest known occurrence of it, and the suggestion has been made that it may have originated in the Celtic church. A field is sown and reaped in a miraculously short time, in order to baffle the pursuers who believed that the Holy Family had gone far ahead. A man who was reaping the corn was asked whether he had seen people pass that way. *Yes*, said he, *I saw them when I tilled this open meadow, which you see being reaped.* And the children of Cain turned back. Indeed, the poets doubtless had an abundance of such lore.

The miracle of the virgin birth is given prominence. Gruffudd ab yr Ynad Coch (c.1280) tells us that Christ was born on a Sunday; likewise Gruffudd ap Maredudd (c.1350–90), who declares that Sunday also was the day of the baptism of Christ, of the miracle at Cana, and the feeding of the Five Thousand. The major events in His life are referred to, and notably His passion. Einion ap Gwalchmai (c.1203–23) refers to the piercing of Christ's left side (HEN GERDDI . . ., 66, 56), while Gruffudd ab yr Ynad Coch describes His coming on the Day of Judgement in exactly the same condition as He appeared on the Cross:

> *A'r gwaet gyn iret a'r dyd y croget,*
> *A'e dwylaw ar llet wedyr llidyaw;*
> *A'r gwaet yn ffrydyev ygkylch y vronneu,*
> *A'e holl welieu heb eliaw;*
> *A'e goron yn drein, ac ynteu yn gelein,*
> *A'e benn yn angkrein wedyr greinnyaw;*

> *Ac ol ffowylleu ar y ystlysseu,*
> *Yr gwneuthur angheu a phoen idaw*
>
> *(With the blood as fresh as the day He was crucified,*
> *With His hands spread out inflamed;*
> *With the blood in streams around His breasts,*
> *And all His wounds left untreated,*
> *With His crown of thorns, and He himself a corpse,*
> *With His head hanging and downcast;*
> *With the marks of whips on His sides,*
> *(Designed) to cause Him death and torment.)*
>
> (ibid., 94.15–22)

Next to Christ and His Holy Mother in the affection of the people came the saints, both native and catholic. The Crusades and contact with the East had doubtless helped to foster devotion to saints and relics. Gwynfardd Brycheiniog (c.1175–80) seeks David's intercession. He had faith in the saint's power:

> *Kanys dichawn Dewi nys dichonwyf,*
> *Gwnaed eiryoled ym am a archwyf*
>
> *(Since Dewi can do that which I can not,*
> *May he make intercession on my behalf for what I seek.)*
>
> (ibid., 46.79–80)

We find Llywelyn Fardd (c.1150–75) making reference to help from David *(porth Dewi,* ibid. 81.9), and in another poem he declares how right it is to praise Cadfan *(moli Kaduan,* ibid. 87.93). Odes to saints were composed by Gwynfardd Brycheiniog —David, Cynddelw—Tysilio, and Llywelyn Fardd —Cadfan. Stories about the Welsh saints, their lives and deeds (all wondrous and wonderful) seem to have been in circulation in the late eleventh and twelfth centuries. This was the time when their LIVES were written, originally in Latin, an important and valuable collection of which is to be found in the British Library MS Cotton Vespasian A xiv, compiled towards the end of the twelfth century, probably at Monmouth. These LIVES, written some five or six hundred years after the time of the saints themselves, should in no wise be regarded as historical works. They were composed in order to extol the name and fame of the saints, more especially as a means of ensuring the position and prestige of the churches with which they were associated. And not only among the Welsh. Normans in south Wales were vitally concerned with the interests and with the history of churches within their newly won lands. It is clear that the poets knew much of the lore associated with these saints. This they may have obtained either directly or indirectly from the LIVES, but more probably from an oral source or sources, upon which the written LIFE also must have in part drawn.

Other forms and subjects in the religious literature of this time are derived from such lore, much of it general to Christendom, and in some cases ultimately traceable to a written source. In many languages we find portrayed the 'signs' before Domesday, presented in a sequence of seven or fifteen. Different versions of the theme are found, e.g. the Comestor, Voragine, and Pseudo-Bede, and they were thought originally to derive from a lost book by St Jerome entitled ANNALES HEBRAEORUM. In Welsh they occur in both prose and metrical forms. In a metrical form we find them in the WHITE BOOK OF RHYDDERCH and in the RED BOOK OF HERGEST, and both versions were published by Henry Lewis in HEN GERDDI ..., 89–93. According to the Red Book, Llywelyn Fardd was the author. On the fifteenth day someone by the name of Gwyn is addressed:

> *Gwyn, gwarandaw y synnwyr*
> *A draetha llyfreu mor llwyr,*
> *Gwyrtheu goleu gwelhattor,*
> *Dyrcheuit mor hyt awyr*
>
> *(Gwyn, listen to the meaning*
> *Which books relate so fully,*
> *Miracles will clearly be seen,*
> *The sea will rise to the sky.)*
>   (ibid., 89–90)

Later poets were also attracted by this theme, for example Dafydd Nanmor (c.1450–80), in a series of *englynion*.

People in general were doubtless acutely concerned with this run up to the Day of Doom, as they must have been with that Day itself. It was a day to be dreaded, and one is not surprised to find it a common subject among the poets throughout the medieval period and later. We may take as an example a poem in the Book of Taliesin entitled *Yrymes Detbrawt (Prophecy of the Day of Judgement)*, which is printed in HEN GERDDI ..., 11–13. In this the poet expressed the oft-repeated view that the Lord has no peer, that it was He who created us. When He comes on the Day of Judgement, there will be wind and sea and fire, lightning and thunder. When the Father descends with His retinue, and the trumpets sound in the four corners of the world, the people of the world *(llwyth byt)* will be burned to ashes. There is a graphic account of the actual judgement, when the dead rise from their graves and Christ addresses all, innocent and guilty:

> *Y sawl a uo meu, ymchoelant o deheu,*
> *A digonwy kamwed, ymchoelant y parth gled*
>
> *(Those who are mine will turn to the right,*
> *Those who committed wrong will turn to the left side.)*
> (ibid., 12.45–56)

Those who drove Him to the Cross He invites to feel His wounds. No pardon is in store for them despite their protestations,

> *A wledic, ny wydyem pan oed ti a grogem*
>
> *(O Lord, we knew not it was Thou we were crucifying.)*
> (ibid., 13.68)

Various views of the Day of Judgement are expressed in the poetry of the period. Christ would be accompanied by the Twelve Apostles, who would take part in the Judgement, which would be held on the Mount of Olives or in the Valley of Jehoshaphat JOEL 3:12 (between the Mount of Olives and Jerusalem). There would be 847 saints with Christ, according to a poem in the Black Book (ibid. 5–14). He would be attended also by the angels, and the archangel Michael is described as carefully weighing in the balance men's virtues and sins. Gruffudd ap Maredudd and Siôn Cent thought it would take place on a

Sunday, but according to Iolo Goch and others Friday would be the day. The whole human race would be brought to judgement, men (and doubtless women) from earth, as well as from heaven and hell. All would appear at the same age, the age at which Christ suffered. Madog ap Gwallter (c.1250) desires a mark on his face, in order not to suffer the punishment of the guilty (cf. REV. 9:4):

Dot not y'm hwynep a'm hadneppych

(Put a mark on my face that Thou mayest recognize me.)
(ibid., 104.76)

For those in search of heaven, it was realized that the Cross and the blood on it brought deliverance:

O'r croc creuled y deuth guared i'r vedissyaud

(From the bloody cross there came deliverance to the world.)
(ibid., 3.14)

Heaven was purchased for us by Christ:

Y nef a brynodd i ni

(Heaven did He buy for us.)
(IOLO GOCH AC ERAILL, 98.25)

It is the true home of virgins, and the way to attain it is to forsake the joys of this life. It has, of course, to be sought:

Nid ew rotir new i'r neb nvy keis

(Heaven will not be given to him who seeks it not.)
(HEN GERDDI ..., 42.75)

The delights and attractions of nature are there:

Myn y mae meillon a gulith ar tirion

(Where there are clovers and dew on lands.)
(ibid., 8.73)

It is a place of joy, and the blessed see God. It is an endless feast:

Keisset bop dedwyd y wled ny deruyd

(Let all the blessed seek the feast that endeth not.)
(ibid., 79.37)

and is located somewhere 'above':

Y sydd uwchlaw haul a ser

(Which is above sun and stars.)
(MYVYRIAN ARCHAIOLOGY ..., 342 a 9)

It resounds with praise, and is without sin *(lle dibechawt)*, without sickness, without night. Its delights will be enhanced by the heavenly host, and its occupants will always be young; according to Siôn Cent no one there will be over thirty (IOLO GOCH AC ERAILL, 274.3–4).

Such are some of the things the poets have to tell us about heaven. Then, there was the shattering realization that those required to 'turn left' eventually had to endure the torment and torture of hell. The thought of hell and its depravity doubtless occupied the minds of the poets and others during this period, and we find it vividly portrayed, often with concentration on gruesome details. Literary authors at all times seem to have had more success with descriptions of hell than of heaven. From the Gogynfeirdd we may take a poem by Gruffudd ab yr Ynad Coch, found in the RED BOOK OF HERGEST and printed in HEN GERDDI ..., 98–100. He begins by referring to Christ as the one who can lead us to a confession of our sins and to penance, to avoid the torments of hell. Woe is declared for those who persist in their sins; such people are categorized and enumerated: the perjurer, the thief, the deceiver, the miser, the proud, the glutton, the traitor, he who neglects the masses of Christ, he who offends against mother and father. Woe unto him that he was born. There is a reference to the seven deadly sins and the five (lost) ages of the world. We are told of the visit of the son of God to the entrance of hell, to smite the unhappy serpent in its jaws (a visit recorded in the Gospel of Nicodemus). Here some ghastly scenes were witnessed:

> *There were boiling there behind those bars*
> *Souls in cauldrons, seven hundred thousand,*
> *And sleet and snow, and serpents and lions,*
>   *And none knew respite from his pain;*
> *And nails keen-pointed, and devil horned,*
>   *With sharp horns hideous upon his heels ...*
> (Trans. HISTORY OF WELSH LITERATURE, 56)

And it goes on and on. Later the Glamorgan poet Casnodyn presents equally grim portrayals of the physical torments of hell. Such descriptions doubtless reflect what was genuinely believed at the time. Sinners would naturally be very grief-stricken, but there was now no escape. Hell was the place for them, a definite place, as the Church affirmed, whose location, however, is not divulged. We are told that it was a great swamp where walking would not be possible. It is also described as deep, and dark. Hell was a place of extreme heat, but it could also be bitterly cold and wet, with snow and ice, frost and rain. Above there is mention of sleet and snow; and cf. further,

> *Eiry, ya, a rew, a ruthyrwynt glew, a glaw dinev;*
> *A gwaeth heuyt oed odef cryt mywn crawn bylleu*
>
> *(Snow, ice and frost, and a strong boisterous wind, and*
>   *pouring rain;*
> *And worse was it also to suffer fever in pools of pus.)*
>   (HEN GERDDI . . ., 102.46–7)

Altogether a shambles, thoroughly hideous and uninviting, a place to be avoided at all costs. Avoidance of hell was a dominant consideration which controlled people's attitude and behaviour.

Small wonder, then, that a common theme among the poets is repentance, regret and remorse for sins and ignoble behaviour. The picture of hell must often have served as a deterrent; ever since they abandoned their Celtic gods, the Welsh never took much pride or pleasure in the heroic ideal. Cynddelw wants to feel repentance for his sin (ibid. 27.10). Another poet emphasizes regret at having loved the world. Note his repetition of the word *ediuar*:

Ediuar gennyf ediuar
Caru byd anglyd anglaear

(*Repentant am I, repentant*
For having loved a comfortless, wretched world.)
(ibid., 80.1–2)

Einion ap Gwalchmai (c.1203–23) speaks of the tears of reconciliation:

Herwyt da greuyt, dagreu dadolwch
Dydelwynt yn hydyr hyt uyg grutyeu

(*In accordance with good religion, may the tears of reconciliation*
Roll strongly down my cheeks.)
(ibid., 65.13–14)

A nameless poet urges redress for wrong committed:

Diwyccom-ne a digonhom o gamuet

(*May we make redress for all the wrong we have done.*)
(ibid., 4.11)

Before entering the grave, and after indulging in steeds and wine and women, the poet says that he sleeps not, and thinks about his end:

Ny chisgaw, gobwyllaw o'm diwet
(ibid., 4.17)

A type of repentance poem, displaying some notable features is the *marw-ysgafn* (*death-bed*), which reminds us of the Middle English penitential. Here the poet presumes to express his feelings in his final (and finest) hour, repentance and remorse, and a desire for forgiveness and reconciliation. While at the time of composition such feelings must have been more imaginary than real, one is occasionally impressed by a note of sincerity. Meilyr Brydydd (c.1100–37), one of the earliest of the Gogynfeirdd, composed such a poem (ibid. 21–22). He admits that he often received from mortal kings *(breuawl rieu)* gold and silk in return for praise, but now as he approaches the end of his worldly life, he wants to join the company of the saints on Bardsey, where it is reputed that twenty thousand of them are at rest, and where

> *The Maker who made me will welcome me*
> *Among the pure flock, the people of Enlli*
> (Trans. ibid. 22.37–8)

'Death-bed' poems were composed also by Cynddelw, and by a later poet Bleddyn Fardd (c.1257–85). Subsequently, they are not found as such, but poetry in a similar vein does occur. We have a 'confession' poem by Gruffudd ap Maredudd (c.1350–90). Llywelyn Goch ap Meurig Hen (c.1350–90) composed an *awdl-gyffes* or 'recantation' in which he makes a line-by-line comparison between God's goodness and his own sins. Guto'r Glyn (c.1445–75), apparently not a particularly religious man, has a poem *Ystyriaeth Bywyd*, which could be described as a *marw-ysgafn*, although it is innocent of any great depth of feeling. Finally, we may refer to the 'confession' of Ieuan Brydydd Hir (c.1450), an uniquely penitent sinner.

The question of sin, of course, looms large in the thoughts of the poets. They knew of the seven deadly sins, and it does not surprise one to find a poet declare that,

> O pechaud kin braud pryderaw

> *(Of sin shall I think before (the Day of) Judgement.)*
> (ibid., 8.12)

A later poet, Madog Dwygraig (c.1370), is apparently anticipating modern thinking when, in confessing his sins, he seems to refer to them as 'loads of emptiness' (THE POETRY IN THE RED BOOK OF HERGEST, 1280.1–2).

In many a poem we find the poet asking for mercy *(trugaredd)*; for example Gwalchmai (c. 1130–80):

> *A'm trugarawc Arglwyt trugarhaed wrthyf,*
> *A mi y wrthaw na'm gwrthoded*

> *(And my merciful Lord, may He have mercy on me,*
> *And not cast me from him.)*
> (HEN GERDDI . . ., 26.107–8)

Meilyr ap Gwalchmai (c.1170–1220), one of the two Gogynfeirdd to whom religious poems only are ascribed, begins one of his poems with the words,

> *A'm bo y gan Duw, a'm bo trugared*

> *(May I obtain mercy from God, may I obtain mercy.)*
> (ibid., 57.1)

Protection is sought from the King by Elidir Sais (c.1190–1240), who may have sojourned in England, and who had some knowledge of ecclesiastical literature:

> *Differ vi, vy Ri, rwyf ysbrydawl*
>
> *(Protect me, my King, spiritual leader.)*
> (ibid., 71.3)

from the severe, fearful penance of the pain of hell:

> *Dygyn enbyd benyd boen vfernawl*
> (ibid., 72.6)

Gruffudd ab yr Ynad Coch seeks protection from Father, Son and Holy Spirit, the Cross, Mary, Peter, the Four Evangelists, John (the Baptist), the Martyrs, Michael and Gabriel (ibid. 97.3–98.36). According to another poet, such protection was obtained when God took flesh:

Dolur eghirith Duv a'n diffirth ban kymirth cnavd

(From huge affliction God protected us when He took flesh.)
(ibid., 3.12)

And finally redemption, salvation and deliverance, which can only be obtained with Christ's help:

> *Duw breinhyawc a brynwys y garant*
> *O'r poeneu a'r pechawt a wnaethant*

*(The noble God redeemed His kinsmen
From the pains and sin they committed.)*
(ibid., 60.5–6)

and later, Siôn Cent (c.1400–30):

*Iesu o gyfraith Foesen
Yn brid a'n prynodd ar bren*

*(Jesus from the law of Moses
At much cost redeemed us on a tree.)*
(IOLO GOCH AC ERAILL, 258.3)

According to Cynddelw (c.1155–1200), He brought us from perdition when He was wounded:

A'n dug o gyfrgoll pan archolled
(HEN GERDDI, 42.55)

Cynddelw asks for salvation from *the King of all people (Brenhin pob gwerin,* ibid. 41.33), while Gwalchmai speaks of Christ as *the hero who has delivered us (gwr arwr a'n rywarawd* ibid. 69.32). Madog ap Gwallter (c.1250), a friar possibly from Llanfihangel Glyn Myfyr, another of the Gogynfeirdd to whom religious poems only are ascribed, confesses his weakness, expresses a desire to be strong, and requests that the Lord be his sustainer, from whom he seeks deliverance and protection:

*Gwaret arnaf, Naf, nawd a'm rodych,
Gwann wyf, ymnerthwyf, vy neirthyat vych*

*(Deliver me, Lord, lend me protection,
I am weak, may I be strengthened, be Thou my sustainer.)*
(ibid., 102.1–2)

Let him not place him on his left side, but rather on his right:

> *Ar y llaw deheu y'm lleheych*
> (ibid., 105–82)

Penance is the safeguard against the torments of hell; it was a sacrament, not to be neglected:

> *I gymryt penyt rac poeneu uffern*
> *Ac affeith pechodeu*
>
> (*To take penance against the torments of hell*
> *And the consequence of sins.*)
> (ibid., 98.7–8)

One way of avoiding the torments of hell was to secure burial in a saint's cemetery. So Gwynfardd Brycheiniog tells us in his ode to David:

> *A el y medrawd mynwent Dewi*
> *Nyd a yn uffern, bengwern boeni*
>
> (*He who enters the grave in the cemetery of Dewi*
> *Will not enter hell, to suffer at the head of the bog.*)
> (ibid., 48.166–7)

While this does not, of course, accord with Christian teaching, it does accord with the material interests of a church. Burial fees were a fruitful source of revenue, and the advantage of burial in a certain cemetery was something to be advertised.

A recurring theme in Welsh, as in other languages, was the dialogue or dispute between

Body and Soul on the question of death. This theme, which derived ultimately from Egypt, is found in most European languages, and in Welsh it occurs in various forms throughout our period. The BLACK BOOK OF CARMARTHEN contains the earliest example of it in Welsh, in a poem exhibiting some rare and early linguistic features. First there is the introduction, which is followed by severe censure from the Soul:

> *Gwae tidi hewid pir doduid im bid,*
> *Onid imwaredit o'r druc digonit*
>
> *(Woe to thee also that thou hast come into the world,*
> *Unless thou dost rid thyself of the evil thou doest.)*
> (ibid., 6.12–13)

The Body is peremptorily told to think of its Soul:

> *Corph diffid direid, gobuill o'th eneid*
>
> *(Faithless, ill-fated body, have regard for thy soul.)*
> (ibid., 6.19)

He did not attend to his devotions:

> *Ni cheuntost-e pader, na philgeint na gosper*
>
> *(Thou didst not sing the Paternoster, or matins or vespers.)*
> (ibid., 6.31)

And he did not respect objects or places of worship:

> *Ni phercheist-e creirev na lloc na llanev*

(Thou didst not respect relics, or monastery or churches.)
(ibid., 7.38)

The Body replies briefly by protesting that it is of the earth, and mentions the seven elements, five of which are named; fire, earth, wind, mist, flowers, which remind us of 'Canu y Byd Mawr' in the BOOK OF TALIESIN 79.11–13, where they are likewise enumerated.

The Body's *apologia* is entirely ignored by the Soul in the final section, where there is reference to union after separation. At the Resurrection three hosts will be brought before Jesus:

Dygettawr y tri llv rac drech drem Iessu

(The three hosts will be brought before the gaze of the eye of Jesus.)
(ibid., 7.67)

Two of these are destined for heaven, the other for hell. The two destined for heaven consist of *llu guirin guinion*, the pure and holy, and *llv arall brithion*, the doubtfuls who nevertheless are eventually united with the former.

When we come to the fourteenth century, we find ourselves at the dawn of a new era in Welsh poetry. We move from the poets of the Princes to the Poets of the Nobles or *Uchelwyr* (c.1300–1650), where we encounter some new features, although they did not appear overnight. There was the final loss of political independence in 1282, along with other major changes and tendencies which resulted in the main from mighty outside influences flooding into Wales. The Princes left a void, which for many centuries was to be filled by Nobles, as well as by some well-disposed clerics, bishops and abbots of monasteries (more especially those of the Cistercians), who now became the custodians and patrons of Welsh literature. The monastery could provide a good table as well as solace and repose for poets and others towards the end of life. The fifteenth-century poet Gutun Owain described the Cistercian house of Maenan as a model of hospitality. A new metre, the *cywydd*, was developed and became popular, and a new system known as *cynghanedd*, consisting of internal rhyme and alliteration, became fixed and regular. Furthermore, the language was much simplified and moved closer to ordinary, everyday speech. Such developments are associated with a number of poets, notably Dafydd ap Gwilym (c.1320–80), one of the greatest Welsh poets of all time. He in particular introduced new themes, concerned with love and nature. Not unrelated to all this is a certain shift of attitude to religion. No longer did it command total reverence. Dafydd himself was not averse to taking it and the Church as a theme for jesting. He sends a love messenger to the nunnery of Llanllugan. After all, the freedom of field and forest is to be preferred to the seclusion of the monastery, and the art of the poet is equal to that of the preacher. Note his dispute with the Grey Friar in a well-known *traethodl*:

> *God is not so cruel, friend,*
> *As old dotards would pretend.*

He'll never damn a gallant lad
For love of matron or of maid . . .
From heaven come mirth and jollity,
But out of hell all misery.
Pleasure grows from poet's song
For sick and whole, old and young.
We have equal warrant each,
I to write verses, you to preach.
As you your trade of begging ply,
So I my trade of minstrelsy.
(Trans. A History of Welsh Literature, 107)

Here we find reflected the other reaction and response to man's mortality. Dafydd sends a girl to St David's to do penance for killing him with her love; in another poem he asks Dwynwen, the patron saint of lovers, to deliver him from the pains of love. Let it not be thought, however, that he was in any way ignorant of the practices and institutions of the Church, and Sir Thomas Parry is right to remind us of the use he made of words and expressions, such as altar, gospel, wafer, chalice, lesson, sacring bell, raising the host, which, along with others, were employed, not to pursue and promote any religious theme, but to enhance and enrich the poet's imagery in his portrayal of the world of nature. A thrush-cock and a nightingale sing together; they are two priests celebrating mass. In a *cywydd*, addressed to his mistress Morfudd, he denies that he ever was a monk. He describes the Star that leads him to her house. She is *this pearl of Mary, the consecrated wafer of heaven's roof*. When he goes to church in Llanbadarn, he can hardly have been in earnest about his devotions:

> *Â'm wyneb at y ferch goeth*
> *A'm gwegil at Dduw gwiwgoeth*
>
> (*With my face towards the fine girl*
> *And my back towards God sublime.*)
>   (GWAITH DAFYDD AP GWILYM, 130.21–2)

Dafydd, however, could hardly be described as a rebel; his poems abound with references to God, Christ and his Holy Mother. He also composed a few religious poems, to Christ, to the Trinity, the Mass (based on the Latin canon), and one to a picture (on wood) of Christ and the Apostles, an art form of which there is increasing evidence in Wales at this time. In one poem Dafydd even says that he is *gŵr â chorun* (*a man with a tonsure*), which seems to imply that at one time he had qualified for minor religious orders.

Developments and shifts there certainly were at this time, with the claims of secular life and the pleasures of the senses becoming unashamedly more to the forefront. From the fourteenth century the religious life seemed to become increasingly less attractive, and the anti-clerical spirit more blatant. We note, for example, poems by Iolo Goch (c.1340–98) abusing friars, and also, for that matter, his highly original and unconventional poem praising the labourer, who is described as honest, upright, unassuming:

> *Nid bywyd nid byd heb ef*
>
> (*There is no life, no world, without him.*)
>   (IOLO GOCH AC ERAILL, 79.24)

A poet like Dafydd Nanmor (c.1450–80) could and did burlesque the confessional, and ask for the power to resurrect a maiden, as Jesus had raised Lazarus. A far smaller proportion than before of the total output of poetry is concerned with religion. However, the old time-honoured themes and subjects continued to engage the mind and the muse of the poets who followed the earlier Gogynfeirdd, namely the later Gogynfeirdd (c.1300–1400) and the *cywydd* poets (c.1350–1650). They sang to God, Christ, the Trinity, the Mass, and sought to describe the Day of Judgement, hell, etc. There was no lack of concern for the obvious decline in standards and ideals, and in the authority of the Church. Nevertheless, in this later poetry there is generally apparent some easing of the intensity, earnestness and conviction of earlier works, as well as evidence of more extensive knowledge and literacy, of widening horizons and of an acquaintance with a greater variety of art-forms. As the poetry of the Gogynfeirdd represented a blend of two cultures, so did the work of these poets, produced as it was by the impact of European on native Welsh life. There must also have been more travel by poets between different parts of the country. One is reminded here of a poem, again by Iolo Goch, consisting of an altercation between Soul and Body, where the Soul mentions people and places in his journeying all over Wales (ibid. 76–8).

Reverence for the Virgin Mary continued unabated. There was a clearer defining of doctrine regarding her as well as lyrical expressions of intense devotion. Iolo Goch, who like Dafydd ap

Gwilym may have been in minor orders, describes her as,

> *Ein eurchwaer, ac yn erchi*
> *Nef a thrugaredd i ni*

> (*Our golden sister, (and) seeking*
> *Heaven and mercy for us.*)
>
> (ibid., 73.20–1)

She was hailed as *Domina Mundi, Regina Celi* and *Imperatrix Inferni*. According to one poet, who waxes eloquent also on her father Joachim and her mother Anna, the conception of Christ in her womb is to be compared to the passage of the sun's rays through glass. The one God gives ear to her entreaties:

> *A'r Unduw ef a wrendy*
> *Neges y frenhines fry*

> (*And the One God listens*
> *To the message of the Queen above.*)
>
> (ibid., 96.29)

A popular theme were the joys of Mary (the Annunciation, Nativity, etc.), which were contrasted with the sadness of the world. Several poems were composed to her by Gruffudd ap Maredudd (c.1350–90), one of the foremost poets of his time, whose religious verse is noteworthy for its imagery, its freshness and vigour. She is described as a star, and as the mother of peace and mercy. He pleads with her for help to overcome his failings. How different is she from our first mother, which makes him play on the letters

EVA/AVE, showing how their roles were reversed. Hywel Swrdwal (c.1430–60), one of the professional poets whose concern for religion was paramount, expresses his deep affection for her in three of his poems.

Later poets, notably Hywel Dafydd ab Ieuan ap Rhys (c.1450–80), were moved to describe her physical appearance, and to elaborate on her golden tresses. In the fifteenth century her cult enjoyed increasing vogue, and over the medieval period she had grown to represent the tender and compassionate aspects of the Christian religion. She was the great mediatrix, interceding for souls at Christ's side.

Sometimes during the fourteenth century there was produced (possibly in Glamorgan) GWASANAETH MEIR, a Welsh metrical translation of the *Officium Parvum Beatae Mariae Virginis*, Office of the B.V.M., in a version similar to the Dominican Use. It contains translations of twenty-eight psalms (one of which is in prose) and other verses of scripture, in fact a larger number of translated scriptural excerpts than in any text of this period. It was one of the most important devotional works of the Middle Ages, and seems intended especially for the layman in private devotion, and later as part of the daily duty of the secular clergy. It is unique in that we have in the Welsh work a translation (or adaptation) into poetry in both strict and free metres, whereas most religious texts were translated into prose. In it *cynghanedd* was not as yet fully developed, which seems to indicate that it was produced before the middle of the century. GWASANAETH MEIR was edited by Professor Brynley F. Roberts, mainly from Shrewsbury School MS XI (c.1400), which contains the earliest copy. Here are the opening lines:

> *Hanpych gwell, Veir, gyflawn o rat; Duw gyda thi:*
> *bendigeit wyt ym mhlith y gwraged; a bendigedic*
> *yw ffrwyth dy groth di, Iesu, Amen.*

> *(Hail, Mary, full of grace; God is with thee:*
> *blessed art thou among women; and blessed*
> *is the fruit of thy womb, Jesus, Amen.)*

A devotional work in prose, which may be dated to the middle of the fifteenth century, is PYMTHEG GWEDDI SAN FFRAID *(Fifteen Prayers of St. Brigit)*, which consists of meditations on the passion of Christ, resulting in terrifying visions of suffering and real torment for him/her who meditates. It is attributed to St Brigitta of Sweden (1303–73). Another devotional work of about the same time, possibly a little earlier, was EMYN CURIG FERTHYR *(the Hymn of Curig the Martyr)*, a hymn of the kind known as *lorica*, in which was sought the protection of the Trinity against danger or disaster.

The poets became increasingly attached to the saints. Invocations of saints are common, and their lives and exploits are recounted with relish. Ieuan ap Rhydderch (c.1430–70), who came from the vale of Aeron in Ceredigion, sang to St David and his shrine. He obviously knew the LIVES of the saints as well as other religious works of the period. Unlike most of his fellow-poets, he must also have known Latin (and French), and may have been a graduate of Oxford. In his ode to

Mary we find a mixture and blend of Latin and Welsh in *cynghanedd*. Other poets who sang to St David were Dafydd Llwyd o Fathafarn (*c*. 1420–1500), that committed Lancastrian who produced so much prophetic verse, and also Lewis Glyn Cothi (*c*.1455–85), one of the important poets of the fifteenth century. Naturally, the more prominent among the saints got pride of place. Beuno, a north Wales saint associated with Clynnog Fawr in Arfon, is the subject of a *cywydd* by Rhys Goch Eryri (*c*.1385–1448), who deals in the main with the saint's death and the vision of heaven experienced by him (IOLO GOCH AC ERAILL, 320–3). As for other saints, we could mention again Dafydd Llwyd o Fathafarn, who sang to Tydecho, patron saint of Mallwyd, and Lewis Glyn Cothi who sang to Llawddog. Iorwerth Fynglwyd (*c*.1500), who was born at St Bride's Major in Glamorgan has a poem to St Bride, while St Illtud is the subject of a *cywydd* by one of the most distinguished Glamorgan poets in his day, Lewis Morgannwg (*c*.1520–50).

Old religious centres were much venerated. Gruffudd ap Dafydd (*c*.1300) has a poem in praise of the well of Cedig. An unknown author composed a *cywydd* to Ffynnon Wenffrewi, in which he says,

> *Ennaint rhag pob haint yw hi*
>
> (*A cure for every ailment is she.*)
>   (ibid., 104.18)

Ieuan Brydydd Hir and Tudur Aled (*c*.1480–1525) also have poems to Gwenffrewi. Some went on pilgrimage to centres further afield. Santiago de Compostella in Spain was quite an attraction despite the perilous sea voyage. Gruffudd Gryg (c.1360–1410) composed a poem to the moon, based on his experience as a pilgrim voyaging from there. We learn from Lewis Glyn Cothi how Dafydd ap John of Gower had gone to Rome in search of parchment pardons. Robin Ddu (c.1450) wrote a poem to commemorate his pilgrimage to Rome in 1450, and Huw Cae Llwyd (c.1457–1504) has a *cywydd* to the relics at Rome he saw during the Jubilee year of 1475, among them a piece of the Cross:

> *Mae o'r Groes a droes yn dri,*
> *Oes, darn y bu Grist arni*
>
> *(There is from the Cross which became three,*
> *Yes, a piece on which Christ lay.)*
> (GWAITH HCLL, 83.77–8)

The Passion of Christ and the Cross continued to attract the attention and devotion of the poets. There was intense meditation on this, and on the Resurrection, as well as on the Harrowing of Hell; individual sins and virtues are described in greater detail. There was the same anguished plea for mercy and deliverance from the torments of hell, notably by poets such as Casnodyn (c.1320–40). According to Gruffudd Fychan, the betrayal of Jesus implicated us all, as Judas was 'our kinsman' (*yn car*, THE POETRY IN THE RED BOOK OF HERGEST, 1296.13). Lewis Glyn Cothi has a *cywydd* on the Crucifixion and Resurrection. Siôn Cent refers to the nails driven into His hands and feet, three in all:

D. SIMON EVANS

Hoelio ei ddwylo ryw ddydd,
Hoelio'i draed â hoel drydydd

(*Nailing His hands one day,*
Nailing His feet with a third nail.)
(IOLO GOCH AC ERAILL, 258.11-12)

Five wounds were inflicted on Him on the Cross, and Bleddyn Ddu, Gruffudd ab yr Ynad Coch and Casnodyn speak of the five streams which issued from these wounds. According to tradition in the medieval period, 5466 wounds in all were inflicted on Christ during His Passion. The very many poems on this subject were not unrelated to the roods which were everywhere being erected, and also to the widely familiar Gospel of Nicodemus, with its account of the Harrowing of Hell.

Poets were attracted to the large cross set up in Chester. Indeed, there were numerous poems in the fifteenth century in which the rood was the focus of worship, at Chester, at Welshpool, at Brecon, at Llangynwyd, at Llan-faes, at Tremeirchion. These poems are concerned with Christ's life, His birth and miracles, but they concentrate on His passion. Care is usually taken to acknowledge the rood as a source of physical and spiritual health, with the power to work miracles. It represents a force which captivated the imagination of the poets as well as artists.

Gruffudd ap Maredudd has a long poem to the cross in Chester (MYVYRIAN ARCHAIOLOGY ..., 307-9), in which there are references to the widely known story of the origin of the Cross, familiar also to the author of a Cornish miracle play. The angel in Paradise gave Seth three seeds to put under Adam's tongue after his death. From them grew three rods, of cedar, cypress and pine (signifying Father, Son and Holy Spirit), which were discovered by Moses who then planted them in the earth. There they remained for a thousand years until the time of David, who found them and brought them to Jerusalem, where they took root and grew into one tree, from which a beam was made for the Temple. The Jews, however, realized that the beam was connected with Jesus, took it from the Temple and deposited it in a lake outside the city. It continued to display its miraculous power, and this caused no little annoyance to the Jews, who eventually used it to make the Cross of Christ and those of the two thieves.

There is plenty of evidence that the poets knew this story. Madog Dwygraig (c.1370) speaks of the Cross as,

> *Prenn o hynaf gweal adaf*

> *(A tree from the oldest rod of Adam.)*
> (THE POETRY IN THE RED BOOK OF HERGEST, 1279.15)

Tudur Aled in his elegy to Dafydd ab Edmwnd likens the growth of the latter's muse from the mouth of Dafydd ap Gwilym to that of the tree of the Cross from the mouth of Adam. And Wiliam Llŷn (d.1580) in his elegy to Gruffudd Hiraethog (d.1564) speaks of the rods obtained from the mouth of Adam:

Doeth fardd, felly daw o'th fedd
Ganghennau'r groes gynghanedd

(*Wise bard, thus will there come from thy grave*
The branches of the cynghanedd groes.)
(BARDD. WLL, 214.65–6)

Gruffudd ap Maredudd also knew the story of what happened to the Cross after the Crucifixion. It had been hidden in the earth by the Jews but was later found by St Helena (MYVYRIAN ARCHAIOLOGY ..., 308 a 40). The feast of the Invention of the Cross was celebrated on the third of May. All this serves to remind us of the amount of apocryphal lore on which the poets and others drew.

In most religious verse the didactic element is implicit, but there are poems, more especially in the later period, where it is patently explicit and obvious. Casnodyn includes a version of the Ten Commandments in one of his odes, and they are embodied also in a *cywydd* attributed to Dafydd Ddu Hiraddug. These and others may well have been intended as a useful aid to memory, although the strict metres generally seem hardly suited for that purpose. An important genre in the fifteenth and sixteenth centuries was what has been described as sermon-poetry, which must have contained current pulpit themes. Earlier in the fourteenth century there was composed a poem, possibly by Llywelyn Goch Amheurig Hen (c.1360–90), in which the Skull is given a tongue to preach a sermon to the parish. A mid-fifteenth-century poet, Ieuan Brydydd Hir of Ardudwy, is the author of two fine sermon-poems. One consists of the well-known motif of a conversation between the living and the dead. This occurs in a church, where the living is disturbed by the manifestation of the dead. Then we have a versified form of the traditional questions, *Quis es tu? Quem video?* The dead explains who he is and describes his condition, and he makes clear the moral through timely pronouncement of the traditional statements, *I was as you are*, and *You will be as I am*. The other is a *cywydd* to old age. Poems occur which contain the *Ubi sunt* motif. One such is attributed to Siôn Cent. Attention is concentrated here on the transitory nature of the things of the world. Famous people are named, and the question asked *Where are they now?* Sir Dafydd Trefor, an Anglesey poet, composed such a poem in the early sixteenth century:

> *Mae Samson, galon y gwyr*
> *nerthol, a phle mae Arthur?*
>
> *(Where is Samson, the heart of strong men,*
> *and where is Arthur?)*
>   (*Cefn Coch MSS* 27.15–16)

They have succumbed to death.

The Dance of Death, with its origin in thirteenth-century France, was popular in the late medieval period. It was initially a dance of the dead, which was thought to happen in cemeteries at night in order to entice the living to join them. Later it became a dance of death, the *danse macabre* with Death personified, leading the living to their inevitable end. This served to emphasize the vanity of worldly pleasures in the face of death, and was designed to bring mortal men to repentance. Confined originally to the visual arts, it was later represented in literature also. In Welsh there is no poem about the Death Dance as such, but several references to it occur, and a *cywydd* by a mid-fifteenth century Glamorgan poet, Llywelyn ap Hywel, consists of a poem in which Death is personified:

> *Drud a dig ar droed a dau,*
> *Diyngan y daw angau.*
>
> *(Fiercely and furiously on a foot that is silent,*
> *Without a sound doth Death come.)*
> (Traddodiad Llen. Morg., 31)

Closely linked to the theme of the personification of death is that of life's wheel, which represents man's fate to which he is bound. The wheel turns, and Death shouts at him. Again there is no escape. The expression *rhwymyn rhod* 'wheel's bond' may contain a reference to this theme.

The Black Death in the fourteenth century and the successive visitations of plague made death a grim reality to many, not excluding the poets. The latter often speak of *y farwolaeth fawr* 'the great death'. The fifteenth century north Wales poet, Gwilym ap Sefnyn (c.1440), lost seven sons and three daughters, and another poet, Ieuan Gethin (c.1460) from Baglan in Glamorgan, lost three sons and two daughters as a result of such visitations. Not surprisingly, artists and poets throughout the medieval period expended much thought and energy in meditating upon death, meditation which increased in intensity and poignancy as the Middle Ages wore on. The fourteenth and fifteenth centuries were times of anguish and bitter frustration. Apart from the Black Death there was the Hundred Years War, and in Wales at the beginning of the fifteenth century the Glyndŵr debacle.

It is probably here that we should mention Siôn Cent, that shadowy figure who may have lived in the early part of the fifteenth century (c. 1400–30), and who may have hailed from one of the border areas (Brecon or Hereford). Poems by diverse authors were doubtless attributed to him during the fifteenth century, when the thoughts and beliefs associated with him seemed to prevail generally in European countries. Certainly, this poetry represented something new in Welsh literature, an outlook and a philosophy which could be described as stoic, severe and harsh, with the accent on doom and gloom. Such views had been expressed before, but never with such force and concentration. It treats of the sinfulness of man, of the deceit and transitory nature of the things of the world. Siôn Cent's task as poet is to describe man and the world as they are:

> *Ystad bardd astudio byd*
>
> (*A poet's estate is to study the world.*)
> (IOLO GOCH AC ERAILL, 284.4)

This poet is a realist, indeed a pessimist, who has been described by Saunders Lewis with some justification as the poet of Christian pessimism. Death is the end of life:

> *Gorwedd yw diwedd pob dyn*
>
> *(Lying down is the end of all men.)*
> (ibid. 257.14)

The horrors of the grave and the torments of hell are depicted, and are intended as a warning to repent and reform before the Day of Judgement, which was thought to be imminent. In many countries it was generally believed that the Last Days were approaching, and that Anti-Christ was about to occupy his throne; earthly existence, it was widely thought, would cease in the year 1400.

Siôn Cent's voice was that of the preacher and prophet, of the uncompromising ascetic; his language and diction is as clear and simple as his message. One of his poems is a reflection of the Test of Friendship theme. It is entitled 'Nid oes Iawn Gyfaill ond Un' *(There is no True Friend but One)*, namely Jesus Christ. This theme is represented in medieval English drama, and also in some *exempla*. In another of his poems, 'I Gyffelybu Dyn i Ddiwrnod' *(To Liken Man to a Day)*, we have a theme reminiscent of a fifteenth-century English poem 'This World is but a Vanyte'. Life is compared with the passing of a day, a long confident morning, followed by mid-day and afternoon. In no time night falls and death is nigh. Siôn Cent maintains that the onset of old age should serve as a warning of what is to come. Man should not become too engrossed with the things of the 'little world' *(y byd bach)*, namely earth and existence on it. Uncertain are the things connected with such a life, namely wealth, health, strength, respect. Not so, however, death and the grave, judgement, heaven or hell; they are all certain.

After death, the grave, the body's resting place:

> *Rhy isel fydd ei wely,*
> *A'i dâl wrth nenbren ei dŷ*
>
> (Low indeed will his bed be,
> With his forehead close to the ceiling of his house.)
> (ibid., 289.3–4)

He will not be allowed to rest alone in peace:

> *A thrychant, meddant i mi,*
> *O bryfed yn ei brofi*
>
> (And three hundred, so they tell me,
> Of worms tasting him.)
> (ibid., 257.21–22)

One should not be surprised then at Siôn Cent's diatribes against the sins of the flesh. He is concerned not only with the fate of the body in the grave, but also with the fate of the soul and the Last Judgement. He has a poem 'I'r Farn Fawr' *(To the Great Judgement)*, which will be held on a hill:

> *A'r farn ddig ar fryn a ddaw*
>
> (And the wrathful judgement which shall come on a hill.)
> (ibid., 280.18)

This is a lengthy *cywydd* with some interesting features. The poet enumerates five fires which will follow in the trail of the Son of God:

> *Pum tân a ddaw o'r awyr*
> *O flaen gwaith i flinaw gwŷr*
>
> *(Five fires will come from the sky*
> *Before action to harass men.)*
> (ibid., 280.23-24)

Unlike most other poems on this subject, Christ here addresses the good as well as the evil. He commends the lords of the land for showing mercy, and for dispensing food and drink, clothes and shelter to the needy and weak (ibid., 282.1-8). The *cywydd* ends with a description of heaven as,

> *Llan uchel yn llawn iechyd*
> *O bob digrifwch o'r byd*
>
> *(A church on high, full of health,*
> *Of every pleasure in the world.)*
> (ibid., 283.23-24)

In another *cywydd*, 'Y Ffordd i'r Nef' *(The Way to Heaven)*, Siôn Cent advocates attendance at church and the paying of dues and tithes (ibid., 274.19-24), a duty urged also by later poets of the fifteenth century. Elsewhere, he stresses the importance of not offending God. Nothing is of any avail, if God is offended:

> *Diffrwyth yw rhwng dwy Affrig*
> *I ddyn ei dda a'i Dduw'n ddig*

> *(Useless between the two Africas*
> *To man are his possessions, with his God offended.)*
>   (ibid., 276.25–26)

We have already touched upon Siôn Cent's view of the purpose of poetry, a view essentially different from that of his predecessors, as well as some of his contemporaries. One recalls his dispute with Rhys Goch Eryri on this question, one of the notable disputes in the history of Welsh poetry, to be compared in some respects (though not in all) with those between Cynddelw and Seisyll Bryffwch in the twelfth century, Dafydd ap Gwilym and Gruffudd Grug in the fourteenth, and Edmwnd Prys and Wiliam Cynwal in the sixteenth. Siôn Cent, who according to Saunders Lewis had been influenced by Bacon's new teaching of *scientia experimentalis*, could not accept the bardic tradition of praise, with its Platonic basis. In many ways he reminds us of Gildas back in the sixth century, who made no secret of his contempt for the praises of the poets. In this dispute with Rhys Goch Eryri, Siôn Cent produced a poem in which he satirizes the 'False Muse' *(Yr Awen Gelwyddog)* (ibid., 181–3). There are two kinds of muses *(deuryw awen)*. The one comes from Christ and has been inherited by the prophets:

> *Hon a gafas yn rasawl*
> *Proffwydi a meistri mawl*
>
> *(This did prophets and masters of praise*
> *Obtain with grace.)*
>   (ibid., 181.9–10)

It speaks not falsehood, or the deceit of blandishment or vanity. The other is the false muse of weak claim, which derives from the furnace of hell. It was inherited by the poets of Wales:

> *Hon a gafas, gwŷr hy,*
> *Camrwysg prydyddion Cymry*
>
> *(This did the false arrogance*
> *Of the poets of Wales, impudent men, obtain.)*
> (ibid., 181.15–16)

He expressed his views clearly and unequivocably, at a relatively barren period for Welsh poetry, in the early years of the fifteenth century, a period to be followed by a hundred years of verse of unequalled beauty and elegance. About 1440, there is evidence of a renaissance, a new outlook, in which the Church seems to have played a part, as is evident from the number of priest-poets in that century, and later. The first of the new poets, Maredudd ap Rhys (c.1440) has already been mentioned. He was as gloomy in his view of the state of the world as Siôn Cent was, and declaimed against it no less vehemently.

Evidence for dramatic verse in Welsh is slight, and mainly confined to the end of the medieval period, indeed to the sixteenth century. From that time there are found in manuscript four religious plays, three of which were published in 1939 by the late Dr Gwenan Jones. What there is of such literature belongs to the border areas, more especially (but not exclusively) the northeast, and it clearly reflects the influence of English centres like Chester, Shrewsbury and

Hereford, where such plays were produced. We know little of the actual performance of plays in Wales, and have to remain satisfied with their names and contents. Of course, they contain apocryphal material, and seem to display features similar to those found in continental and English plays, in Chester and elsewhere. Two of them are mysteries, namely the THREE KINGS OF COLOGNE and the PASSION. The first deals with the coming of the *Magi*, the flight to Egypt, and the killing of the innocents. The PASSION seems to consist of two plays, and includes the Trial, Crucifixion and Resurrection, and also the Descent into Hell, the setting up of the watch and the women at the sepulchre. The other two are morality plays. SOUL AND BODY is a dialogue in which each accuses the other of sin. When they part, the soul is snatched away by the Devil. There is also a judgement scene. Michael comes to fight for the soul, but without success. Then come Mary and her Son, and it is saved. The other, the STRONG MAN, which is written in the *traethodl* metre, is a debate between a gentleman—covetous and worldly—and a priest who seeks to persuade him that the goods of the world are of no value, but to no avail. The gentleman falls ill, repents and appeals for mercy. He then dies. The priest dutifully prays for his soul, and the play ends with the servant John making love to the widow, marrying her and squandering her possessions. These plays, which are not mere translations and have features of their own, were probably composed in the latter half of the fifteenth century, or early in the sixteenth. They are meant to be performed, in the churchyard or even in the church itself, as seems suggested by a reference in one of Dafydd ap Gwilym's poems (GWAITH DAFYDD AP GWILYM, 294.5–6). Such a practice may go back to earlier times, and one can refer to the evidence of Giraldus Cambrensis (in 1188) that on the first day of August, the feast-day of St Eluned, in Brecon young men and maidens in the church and in the churchyard sing and dance, and *in full view of the crowds they mimic with hands and feet whatever work they had done contrary to the commandment on Sabbath days.*

The plays would be readily understood, as they are in free metre with no *cynghanedd* and abound with dialect forms. Poems in free metre known as *cwndidau* were also composed, and used as simple religious instruction for the uninitiated. They could, indeed, be described as sermons in song. These again date from the sixteenth century, although it appears that they were first produced in the fifteenth. They belong to south Wales, to Glamorgan and Gwent, and to a lesser degree to Carmarthenshire, and as is to be expected, they consist of an abundance of sermon themes, presented like the plays in a language full of colloquial and dialect forms. One of the themes in them was the passing of the old order. The Roman Church, its theology and ritual, was now being superseded by a new faith, *ffydd Saeson (the faith of Englishmen)*, as described by some. Tomas ab Ieuan ap Rhys of Llandudwg, one of the earlier *cwndidwyr*, genuinely regrets the change *when Rome was set at nought*:

> *Even so was it with the Island of Britain*
> *When Rome was set at nought—*

> *Without prayer or fasting,*
>   *Or penance or absolution,*
> *Or confession or extreme unction,*
>   *Or burial or baptism,*
> *Or censer or blessed wax,*
>   *Or pax, there was no need of it,*
> *Or Cross to recall the Redeemer,*
>   *Or blessed water,*
> *Or Communion of Christ's body,*
>   *'Tis sad we are to lack it*
> (Trans. A HISTORY OF WELSH LITERATURE, 176)

Truly sorrowful and sordid, indicative of the feelings and frustrations of some at this time of change, uncertainty and insecurity.

II

When we come to examine the religious prose of the medieval period, we are struck by some important differences between it and the poetry. Two may briefly be noted. The prose is later than the poetry, and cannot be dated to a time earlier than the middle of the thirteenth century. It is also less 'native', in that it presents little originality in theme and content. With the exception of the LIVES of the native saints, which will be dealt with later, the prose works are based on foreign originals, and consist almost entirely of translations and adaptations from Latin. They reflect very clearly what was taught and read and heard generally by people in the Christian lands of western Europe, where there was a greatly increased output of popular religious prose. We look in vain, however, for Welsh versions of leading religious and philosophical treatises, such as appeared elsewhere in the twelfth century and later, and were intended for the few.

We may start with the first indications of the need felt for presenting certain texts in Welsh. It becomes apparent as early as the thirteenth century that members of the Welsh nobility were taking steps to secure the production of such works. The Athanasian Creed, or *Quicumque Vult*, was translated into Welsh as *Credo Athanasius Sant* by Brother Gruffudd Bola, about whom we know nothing. However, we are in luck that even his name is mentioned to us, because unlike the poets, most of whose names and approximate dates are known, the authors of the prose works for the most part maintain an anonymity which is in keeping with the non-individual, non-distinctive, indeed impersonal nature of their work. In the case of the *Credo*, however, we are not only told the name of the author, but also that of the person for whom it was done, namely Efa, daughter of Maredudd, son of Owain. It was produced for the love of Efa and in her honour (*yr caryat Eua . . . a'e henryded*). Maredudd ab Owain was a great-grandson of the renowned Lord Rhys (d.1197), lord of Deheubarth, who was such a dominating figure in Welsh life in the second half of the twelfth century, with his centre in Dinefwr. Among the many and varied events associated with him, two stand out. One was the founding of the Cistercian monastery at Strata Florida in 1164, which became an important centre and focus of cultural and religious activities for many centuries. The other was the holding of an eisteddfod (the first of its kind) in Cardigan in 1176. There is no lack of evidence that the descendants of the Lord Rhys maintained their interest and involvement in such enterprises for long after his time. His descendant, Maredudd ab Owain, was highly thought of by both poet and chronicler, and on the occasion of his death (in 1265), the latter described him as *the defender of all Deheubarth and the counsellor of all Wales*. Efa was his daughter, and Professor Caerwyn Williams pertinently asks whether she was *a product of the new interest in the education of devout women which, beginning in the twelfth century, had spread rapidly all over Europe*. Be that as it may, there are cases elsewhere of wealthy ladies commissioning vernacular manuscripts. Efa obviously had an intelligent interest in the works translated for her, and Gruffudd Bola had a high enough opinion of her to explain to her what he was aiming at in his translation. It is clear that she could read it, and was anxious to obtain it, but it is equally clear that she was not able to consult the work in the original Latin. Another cleric, Madog ap Selyf, produced translations for Efa's brother, Gruffudd, translations of the CHRONICLE OF TURPIN and of the apocryphon TRANSITUS BEATAE MARIAE. Both Gruffudd Bola and Madog ap Selyf must have been members of a religious house, Strata Florida or Llanbadarn, and other manuscripts at this time were certainly produced at such centres.

As in the case of other vernacular languages, Welsh was now being adopted by the nobility as a literary medium for works whose original language was beyond their ken. One can identify two types of people for whom it was necessary to provide religious and devotional works in Welsh. One was the priest in charge of souls. He required material for the instruction and edification of his flock, who probably could not read any language. The other was the *uchelwr*, who belonged in the main to the lesser gentry, and who now for the first time became literate in Welsh, the only language he knew. Professor G. J. Williams and Sir Idris Foster have both referred to the evidence that members of the nobility commissioned clerics (mostly members of religious orders) to produce for them translations or adaptations of works in Latin or French, works both secular and religious. We have no means of fully knowing the general picture, but there are some specific pieces of evidence which we can mention. In a manuscript of the fourteenth century (written probably towards the middle of that century), known as the BOOK OF THE ANCHORITE OF LLANDDEWIBREFI, there occurs the unusual feature of an introductory note, which informs us about the production of the book:

Gruffud ap Llywelyn ap Phylip ap Trahayarnn o Kantref Mawr a beris yscrivennv y llyuyr hwnn o law ketymdeith idaw, nyt amgen, gwr ry oed agkyr yr amsser hwnnw yn Llandewyureui, y rei y medyanho Duw y heneideu yn y drugared, Amen.
                  anno domini. MCCC. Quadragesime Sexto

(Gruffudd ap Llywelyn ap Phylip ap Trahaearn of Cantref Mawr had this book written by an acquaintance of his, namely a man who was an anchorite at that time in Llanddewifrefi, whose souls may God hold in His mercy. Amen. 1346.)

It is interesting to observe that Gruffudd ap Llywelyn of Cantref Mawr (the area north of the Tywi in Carmarthenshire) was connected with the same family as Efa. His wife, Elen or Eleanor, was the daughter of a grandson of Maredudd ab Owain. THE BOOK OF THE ANCHORITE, consisting entirely of religious texts, in itself constitutes evidence that members of the nobility were commissioning clerics to compile for them collections of Welsh works, in both poetry and prose. The most important manuscript of the medieval period, the RED BOOK OF HERGEST, now in the Bodleian Library at Oxford, has been dated to the period 1375–1425. According to the late Professor

G. J. Williams, it was produced for Hopcyn ap Tomas ab Einion, an *uchelwr* of Ynystawe in Glamorgan. At about the same time (*c*.1400) there was produced another manuscript consisting solely of religious texts, a manuscript in the National Library of Wales at Aberystwyth, known as Llanstephan 27 or the RED BOOK OF TALGARTH. The writing here closely resembles that of large parts of the RED BOOK OF HERGEST, and the suggestion has been made that they were written by the same hand (that of Hywel Fychan) and for the same person. Hopcyn ap Tomas had a brother Rhys, and for him a cleric, Dafydd Fychan of Glamorgan translated the text known as FFORDD Y BRAWD ODRIG *(Brother Odrig's Journey)*, the story of Odoric's travels through Asia in the first half of the fourteenth century. A manuscript consisting of religious texts is Peniarth 5 in the National Library, which forms part of the WHITE BOOK OF RHYDDERCH (*c*.1350), another important medieval manuscript. The Rhydderch here reminds one of Parcrhydderch, Llangeitho in the vale of Aeron, the home of one of the most notable families in Wales at this time. The book may well have been commissioned by them, and produced at Strata Florida or the related Strata Marcella.

It is clear that from the middle of the thirteenth century for a century or so there was considerable activity among some clerics, involved, as they were, in the production of religious prose for instructional and devotional purposes. Such enterprise had the support and patronage of the nobility and the higher clergy, concerned as they must have been with the proper education of the clergy and their flocks, in the only language they understood. Here we must mention the Fourth Lateran Council of the Church held in 1215, and subsequently a Council held at Oxford in 1222 on ecclesiastical administration in England. Both were part of the movement for reform in the Church in the thirteenth century. Bishops were fully aware of the nature and extent of the problem posed by ignorant, even illiterate, clergy, and as a result we find episcopal statutes expounding in a simple manner the essentials of the Christian Faith; the clergy are urged *to instruct their parishioners in these matters, simply and in the vernacular*. The bishops of Llandaff and St David's were present at the Fourth Lateran Council, and its effects must have been felt in Wales. Sir Idris Foster, with his percipient analysis of the situation, draws attention to the appointment of the Dominican, Thomas Wallensis, archdeacon of Lincoln, as bishop of St David's in 1247. He was unquestionably a man of ability and scholarship, with wide and varied experience, who must have been influenced by the movements and tendencies of his time.

A large number of manuscript copies of religious texts, mostly from south Wales, have survived from the late medieval period. One such is HYSTORIA LUCIDAR, or ELUCIDARIUM, found in some twenty-two manuscripts, including the BOOK OF THE ANCHORITE and the RED BOOK OF TALGARTH. It must have proved popular, as it was copied time and time again during the period from the fourteenth century to the eighteenth. There is evidence that it (along with other religious texts from the BOOK OF THE ANCHORITE) was known to the knowledgeable Gruffudd Llwyd of Llangadfan (c.1380–1420), and we know from the evidence of another poet, Dafydd y Coed, that Hopcyn ap Tomas of Ynystawe had a copy. It is a catechistical text presented in dialogue form in three parts—a handbook of the Faith, and a shortened version of a Latin work of the early twelfth century by Honorius Augustodunensis, who has been described as a popularizer of knowledge for the lower clergy. The first part is concerned with God and the Creation until the redemption of the world by Christ. The second deals with various questions relating to sin and its manifestations, in which contemporary problems are discussed and interesting judgements pronounced. One of the questions asked is, *What hope is there for the poets (y gler:* Lat. *joculatores)? None, because with all their might they serve the devil* ... And further, *What hope is there for the merchants (porthmyn)? Little, because it is from deceit, and acts of perjury, and usury, and gain, that they seek almost everything to amass it.* (Trans. THE ELUCIDARIUM AND OTHER TEXTS, 40). The material of the third section is eschatalogical.

Let us next look at some other texts in the BOOK OF THE ANCHORITE, most of which are found also in the WHITE BOOK OF RHYDDERCH (Peniarth MS 5) or in the RED BOOK OF TALGARTH. Another catechistical text in the form of question and answer is *Hystoria Adrian ac Ipotis (Adrianus et Epictitus).* It begins thus:

Pwy hynnac a vynnho dyscu doethinab ac ysprydolyon orchestonn, gwaranndawet ar yr ymdidan a'r amofyn a oruc agkredadwy amherawdyr a uu gynt yn Rufein vawr, a hwnnw a elwit Adrian amherawdyr.

(Whoever desires to learn wisdom and spiritual feats, let him listen to the conversation and the questioning which the unbelieving emperor who was once in great Rome did; and he was called emperor Adrian.)

The answers are provided by a gentle lad named Ipotis, who is endowed with heavenly knowledge and wisdom. This is a version of the *L'Enfant Sage (Wise Child)* legend, which, unlike almost all Welsh religious prose works, may derive from an English prototype.

There are a number of small tracts which seek to expound the creeds and articles of the Church. First, we have in the BOOK OF THE ANCHORITE and in the RED BOOK OF TALGARTH the *Quicumque Vult* or *Credo Athanasius Sant,* in a version different from that in the WHITE BOOK OF RHYDDERCH, already mentioned. *Y Drindawt yn Vn Duw (The Trinity as One God)* is again a short treatise on the Trinity. *Deudec Pwnc y Credo (The Twelve Subjects of the Creed)* occurs in a thirteenth-century manuscript, namely Peniarth 16. *Py delw y dyly dyn credu y Duw (In what way should a man believe in God)* occurs in some twenty-one manuscripts in all. First we have enumerated variations of the formulae in the Creed, followed by a brief account of the nature of love, the Ten Commandments with a commentary, the seven mortal sins, sacraments and deeds of mercy, already referred to. The importance of attending mass is stressed in a short text. *Rinwedeu gwaranndaw Offeren (The Virtues of hearing Mass).* *Pwyll y Pader o dull Hu Sant (The Meaning of the Paternoster according to Hu Sant)* is based on work ascribed to Hugh of St Victor, the distinguished twelfth-century scholar and theologian from Paris. It is an exposition of the Lord's Prayer, presented, clause by clause, and its importance in the main consists of the evidence in it of the development of a Welsh vocabulary for medieval mystical theology. A commentary on the Lord's Prayer attributed to St Augustine occurs in Peniarth MS 16, which also contains a Welsh version of the *Ave Maria*. Another text relating to the Lord's Prayer, in both prose and metrical forms, is entitled *Seith Wedi y Pader (The Seven Prayers of the Paternoster)* (THE POETRY IN THE RED BOOK OF HERGEST, 1366–7) in which it is shown that each petition in the Lord's Prayer serves as an antidote against each of the seven deadly sins. *Am gadw Dyw Sul (On the observing of Sunday)* or *Ebostol y Sul*, is quite explicit in expounding the dire consequences of desecrating Sunday. Payment of tithe is urged. As for him who does not pay, *ef a geiff bar Duw ar y gorff a'e eneit; ac ny wyl buched tragywydawl yn y lle y mae yn gobeithaw y welet (he will get the wrath of God on his body and his soul; and he will not see eternal life in the place where he hopes to see it)*. Here are echoed views expressed by Siôn Cent and others.

These texts and others are indicative of the attempts made to improve the standard of clerical learning. Priests were required to give instruction in subjects such as the Lord's Prayer, the Ten Commandments, the articles of the Creed, the sacraments, etc., and handbooks for such instruction were now available in Welsh. Another text available in Welsh was the one known as *Penityas*, one of the shrift-books produced to aid priests, who were also expected to hear confession and impose penance:

Llyma dechreu Penityas. Gwybydadwy yw mae o'r mod hwn y dyly offeiryat ymdyborthi tu a phechadur a del y gyffessu attaw.

(*This is the beginning of Penityas. It is known that in this manner should a priest deal with a sinner who comes to confess to him.*)

It first appeared c.1400 in Peniarth MS 190, but the original composition must be earlier. It is based largely on a Latin work, SUMMA DE POENITENTIA ET MATRIMONIO by St Raymund de Pennafort, a Spanish canonist of the thirteenth century who produced the first great work of moral theology. The theme of sin became common in the literature of the period, as may be seen in the work of authors such as Langland, and also Chaucer; there were detailed and concrete descriptions of sins as committed by Christians. According to the twenty-first canon of the Fourth Lateran Council, the faithful were obliged to make confession at least once a year, and to take communion at least every Easter.

An important text, somewhat different from the others, is *Kyssegyrlan Vuched* or *Ymborth yr Eneit*, of which twenty-two manuscript copies survive. It is the only clear manifestation in Welsh of erotic mysticism. The Welsh text consists only of the third book, which is divided into three parts:

The first part treats of the vices to be shunned and the virtues to be practised. The second part treats of Divine Love through which God and man are joined together. The third part treats of the pleasant ecstasies which come from that Love, and of the visions which the Holy Spirit gives in the ecstasies and of the nine grades of Angels ... (Trans. Foster)

Sir Idris Foster has demonstrated that *what is basically a manual of practical theology becomes a guide to mystical theology.* The initial stages emphasize the exercise of the deeds of virtue. In the second part the theological assumptions are expounded. Then there follow penance, contemplation, ecstasies, visions and the final *amplexus*, all, however, based on the love of God: *for His Love is the food of our souls ... as God is the life of the soul.* Here the mystical experiences of a Dominican serve as a frame for a picture of the complete process which leads to the vision of God. After penance and continuous prayer there comes an ecstatic vision, reaching its climax in the revelation of the Son of God as a child of twelve years—*Pryt y Mab (The Form or Appearance of the Son)*. The child is described in a long, highly coloured passage, obviously an interpolation, and possibly in origin an independent composition. Here is a section, including some descriptive adjectives, from this passage:

mab *melynnwynn adueindwf* oed val yn oet deudegmlwyd ... penn *gogygrwnn gwedeid* idaw. a gwallt *penngrychlathyr pefyrloyw eureit velynnlliw* arnaw ... a hynny megys ar voe no rychwant o bop tu y'r deu wynep *glaerwynnyon*. a thoryat *pedawlfuryf* ar y gwallt ar y dal ... a'r gwallt oll yn *benngrychlathyr* hyt ar yr yat. ac yno yn benn *llyfynlwys gribedicloyw* vrth gynnwyssaw yr eur goron arnaw. a gwynndal *gwastatlyfyn ehanglathyr mereridliw* idaw
(THE ELUCIDARIUM AND OTHER TEXTS ..., 92)

The adjectives are in italics, and we can see at a glance how frequently they occur, more especially compound adjectives. This, of course, reminds us of the style of the oration *(araith)*, which formed part of the training in the bardic schools, and whose use is displayed in some notable prose works, such as *Culhwch ac Olwen*. While it must be conceded that much of the imagery here acquires significance only when it is placed within the context of earlier medieval religious writing in Latin, it is difficult to escape the conclusion that this part of *Kyssegyrlan Vuched* at least is the 'original' work of a conscious, trained literary artist who was, however, affected by Anglo-Norman influences, as is shown by his choice of words. Note, for instance, *krocket wedeidlwys* as a description of the hair-style, reminding us of Middle English *croket (lock of hair)*.

Then there follow sections in which are prescribed the methods of attaining ecstasy and union. Faith and contemplation are required, and the invoking of the Holy Spirit through the words of the *Veni Creator Spiritus*, with the hymn set to the Welsh metre *rhupunt*. There are, furthermore, indications of the cult of the Holy Name, here clearly an instrument of ecstasy. The work ends, appropriately enough, with a description of the celestial hierarchy, followed by three *englynion*.

It is not possible to trace the immediate source or sources of this important text, the rhetorical richness of its style and the variety of its images. However, in it, as Sir Idris Foster reminds us, *the patient eye can discern the forms and modes of twelfth- and thirteenth-century mysticism*. Unlike most of the works in Welsh left to us from medieval times, this was meant for the few, for members of a religious order, although the more serious among the laity must also have been attracted by it.

Reference has already been made to the apocryphal lore known to the poets. Tales, some of them of early origin, not admitted into the Canon, were in wide circulation during the medieval period. They contained much that was wondrous and wonderful, not dissimilar in this respect to secular tales, and equally improbable. Apocryphal literature and midrash, relating to Biblical history and Biblical characters, is found in a number of prose-texts in Welsh. One is *Efengyl Nicodemus*, representing perhaps two independent translations and occurring in some ten manuscripts in all. It purports to give authentic information about the Resurrection. The Latin *Euangelium Nicodemi*, from which it was translated, consisted of two works, *Acta Pilati (The Acts of Pilate)* and *Descensus Christi ad Inferos (The Descent of Christ to Hell)*, first combined in the fifth century. The *Euangelium Nicodemi*, derived originally from a Greek text, deeply influenced the literature of the medieval period, while the account of Christ's descent into hell made a profound impression also on art in its various forms. He went there, and rescued the elect of the Old Testament, including Adam:

Ac ystynnv y lav a oruc yr Argluyd a dodi aruyd y Groc ar Adaf, ac y seint ef. A chymryt y llav deheu y Adaf, ac ysgynnv o vffernn, a'r holl seint a ymlynassant yr Arglwyd

(And the Lord stretched out His hand and placed the sign of

the Cross on Adam, and His saints. And He took Adam's right hand and ascended from hell, and all the saints followed the Lord.)

We have already observed how familiar the poets were with the story of the origin of the Cross. It is recounted in *Ystorya Adaf (History of Adam)* wrongly known in some mauscripts as *Efengyl Nicodemus*. Another apocryphal tale known to the poets gave the history of the Cross after the Crucifixion. It was *Fal y cafas Elen y Wir Groc (How Helen discovered the True Cross)*, translated from the well-known *Inventio Sancte Crucis (The Discovery of the Holy Cross)*. This Helen/Helena, wife of Constantius, emperor of Rome, was confused with the Elen Luyddog of Welsh legend, or Ellen of the Hosts, the bride of the Roman emperor, Maximus. In Peniarth MS 5 an account of the Crucifixion based on Matthew's Gospel occurs between *Ystorya Adaf* and *Fal y cafas Elen y Wir Groc*, the three clearly intended to serve as one complete story. In the same manuscript we have a text which also takes us back to very early times. It is *Ystorya Adaf ac Eua y Wreic (The History of Adam and of Eve his Wife)*, which derives immediately from a Latin work, although the ultimate source is Jewish. Here we are told how Adam and Eve did penance in the waters of the Jordan and the Tigris, before journeying back to the gates of Paradise, in the hope of obtaining some alleviation to their misery.

We have seen how profound and progressive the effect the cult of Mary had upon the poets. A number of prose-works also relate to her life and work, her gifts and miracles, her role as intercessor, her Assumption. An early text, found in Peniarth MS 14 (c.1250), recounts her miracles, thirty-two of them. By this time, from the twelfth century to the fourteenth and later, adoration of her had breached all bounds of reason and restraint. In her wondrous ways she is described as coming to the rescue of many different people in situations of danger and crisis: a Jewish boy, a pregnant woman, a bishop, a thief, an anchorite, a pope, a scholar, a prostitute, an abbess, a monk, an abbot, a parish priest, an archdeacon, a judge, a husbandman, a prior, a sick man, a merchant, an emperor. The one thing they had in common was devotion and respect for her, which qualified them all for help and succour, despite any other adverse or disqualifying feature.

An account of the Assumption of the Virgin occurs at the end of this text. Other texts and versions of this story, entitled *Esgyniad Mair i'r Nef*, are found, some twelve altogether, and they all derive from versions of the Latin *Transitus Beatae Mariae*. At the end, the Lord Jesus was present with the Virgin and the Apostles, who had assembled for the final act. He embraced them and told them,

'Tangneved yuch, canys y gyt a chui yd wyf vi en wastat hyt en diwed byt.' Ac ar y geiryeu henne, ef a emdyrchavavd en wybren ac a dyrchauwyt e nef. A'r engylyon enteu a dugant y Wynvydedic Ueir e baradwys Duw.

('Peace unto you, because with you I am always till the end of the world.' And with those words He ascended into the sky, *and was raised to heaven. And the angels then brought the Blessed Mary to the paradise of God.)*

Another text relating to Mary gives an account of her life and the infancy of her Son, *Buched Meir Wyry a Mabolyaeth an Harglwyd ni Iessu Grist* or *Mabinogi Iessu Grist*, a work widely known in Wales, not least among the poets. It derived from *Pseudo-Matthaei Evangelium sive liber de ortu beatae Mariae et Infantia Salvatoris*, one version of which may have been composed as early as the sixth century. Here we learn of Mary's parents, Anna and Joachim who had been without child for twenty years. Joachim, who had retired in shame to remote parts, returned at the bidding of the angel to find that his wife had conceived. Anna dedicated her child to the Temple, where she remained until she was fourteen. Then Joseph, a somewhat unattractive, aged figure (described as *saer hen* and as churlish and mean by Hywel Swrdwal), was chosen as her reluctant husband, a choice determined by the miraculous sign of a dove alighting upon his head. Then came the Annunciation by Gabriel of the birth of her son. Her virginity, although in doubt at first, was eventually recognized and acclaimed. Jesus was born, and we have an account of many wondrous deeds performed and gifts displayed by him while still a child, corresponding in part to the stories in Matthew and Luke, but with some startling embellishments and additions. The three earliest texts of this work represent independent translations, of which the one in Peniarth MS 5 only is complete. It bears the title,

Llyma mal y treithir o vuched Meir Wyry, ac o vabolyaeth

an Hargluyd ny, Iessu Grist, herwyd mal y yscriuenwys Matheu euangylystor yn Eurey, a Sein Jeronym o lyuyr Matheu a'e troes o ieith Eurey yn Lladin, trwy adolwyn y gan Chromatius ac Elyodorus.

(*This is how is related the life of the Virgin Mary, and the infancy of our Lord, Jesus Christ, as Matthew the evangelist wrote it in Hebrew, and Saint Jerome from the book of Matthew translated it from Hebrew into Latin at the request of Chromatius and Elyodorus.*)

Peniarth MS 5, along with nine other manuscripts, also contains a copy of *Ystorya Titus Aspassianus (The History of Titus Vespasian)*. This is derived from the Latin *Vindicta Salvatoris*, and tells how Titus and Vespasian came to sack Rome in order to avenge the crucifixion of Christ. Woven into this history is the popular legend of Veronica, the woman reputedly healed by Christ of an issue of blood. She wiped His face with a handkerchief, and on it there remained its imprint which displayed miraculous powers of healing. We are told also of the ultimate fate which befell Pilate after he had been brought before the emperor. He was imprisoned and eventually killed himself, but his body proved difficult to dispose of, a story possibly intended as a gentle reminder that the evil men do live after them! More unseemly and unsavoury episodes in the career of Pilate are recorded in a short text, *Ystorya Bilatus*. There is also recorded a short letter sent by Pilate to the emperor Claudius concerning the crucifixion and resurrection of Jesus. A brief account of the troubled life of the ill-fated Judas occurs in a text entitled *Historia Judas*.

We have already noted descriptions of heaven and of hell, as they were known to the poets. Hell more especially was also known from descriptions given in visions or dreams, reputedly experienced by well-known characters. It was important to quote the evidence of such people, in order to refute agnostics and doubters. *Breudwyt Pawl Ebostol (The Dream of the Apostle Paul)* describes what Paul and also the archangel Michael saw on their visit to hell. They were so shattered that they implored God to let the sinners have Sunday free from turmoil and torment, to allow it as a day of rest. This the Lord conceded, to the relief and joy of the host in hell. When Paul approached the gates of hell, he witnessed unbearable suffering:

Ac yna Pawl a welfas gyr bronn pyrth vffernn deri tanllyt, ac vrth y keinghev pechaduryeit ygkroc; rei onadunt gyr blew y pennev, eraill gyr eu dwylaw, ereill gyr eu breuantev, ereill gyr y tafodeu, ac ereill gyr y breicheu.

(And then Paul saw beside the gates of hell oak-trees burning, and from the branches sinners hanging; some of them by the hair of their heads, others by their hands, others by their throats, others by their tongues, and others by their arms.)

This text is found in some twenty-four manuscripts, and is based on versions of *Visio Sancti Pauli*, a work deriving ultimately from a Greek source of the fourth century.

Such visions proved popular and helped to promote doctrines relating to the Other World, and also Purgatory. It was in them that Dante doubtless found the model for his great work. Another well-known vision was *Purdan Padric (Purgatorium S. Patricii)* found in some seventeen manuscripts. The *Purgatorium* was located in a small island in Lough Derg in county Donegal, where it had been revealed to Patrick that there was a cave in which one could see the torments of Purgatory and the joys of heaven, and be purged of sin. In the middle of the twelfth century c.1153, it was visited by a knight called Owen, who had experience of Purgatory and of heaven, and went on a crusade. A Cistercian monk of Louth, named Gilbert, brought the story back to England, and it was later given literary form (in Latin) by another monk, Henry de Saltereia of Huntingdon, about 1190.

Another work of interest is *Ysbryd Gwidw a'r Prior (The Spirit of Gwidw and the Prior)*, a text in the form of question and answer which occurs in manuscripts of the fifteenth century and later. Gwidw has died (in 1324), and his widow in her grief and frustration has gone to converse with the prior, who asks the spirit of Gwidw questions concerning him, his plight and fate, and also advice on the behaviour and response of the living regarding hours and masses, along with other matters. The spirit suitably responds and expounds, and requests prayers for himself and all the souls in Purgatory. He urges the living to improve their life lest they be lost; then he becomes silent and departs. The pope (John) verifies that he is no longer there, and it is accepted that he has gone to heaven.

In poetry and in prose, as we have seen, the Welsh were greatly attracted by the signs and events preceding the Day of Judgement, also by the coming of Anti-Christ and the Day of Judgement itself. A version occurs in the RED BOOK OF TALGARTH. We may also mention a text found in the British Library MS Cotton Titus D xxii (c. 1430), while another version apparently representing a different translation from Latin is found in Llanstephan MS 2 (c.1450–1500). In this manuscript there occurs another and different text concerned with this subject; here a definite date is given for the end of the world, namely 1365.

Mention has already been made of the Saints and their LIVES. First, the general saints of the Church, whose lives and deeds were of immense interest to all Christians. The LIVES of some of them were translated into Welsh from about the middle of the thirteenth century, mostly chaste and virgin females such as Catherine, Margaret, Mary Magdalen, Martha and Mary of Egypt, doubtless reflecting the new interest in the virgin life and the education of devout women, and in erotic mysticism. All this came with the religious awakening of the twelfth century, which in England produced the great prose book of the ANCREN RIWLE, and one must assume a mystical element in the religious life and literature of Wales at this time. In two early manuscripts, Peniarth 14 (c.1250) and 5, there are copies of *Gvyrthyeu Seint Edmund Archesgob Keint (The Miracles of St. Edmund, archbishop of Canterbury)*, where twenty-four of them are enumerated. In the second half of the fifteenth century we have the LIFE OF ST. MARTIN, translated by Siôn Trefor Hen, and there are also Welsh versions of other LIVES by Hugh Pennant, based upon the collection in the

D. SIMON EVANS

LEGENDA AUREA (c.1255) by the famous Jacobus de Voragine, a work of which the Anglican Morus Kyffin at the end of the sixteen century had such a low opinion. A number of Latin LIVES of Welsh saints, belonging to the late eleventh and twelfth centuries, have survived. Some of these were later translated into Welsh, notably the LIVES of David and Beuno, the Latin original of which is now lost. These LIVES are found in a number of manuscripts, the earliest being the BOOK OF THE ANCHORITE and the RED BOOK OF TALGARTH. Later we find versions of the LIVES of Collen, Llawddog, Ieuan Gwas Padrig, Curig and Gwenffrewi.

It is important to try and appreciate the significance of the Saint and his LIFE in the thought and worship of medieval society. As we are reminded by Professor Caerwyn Williams, who has done so much to improve our knowledge and understanding of religious literature, the people contributed as much to the composition of the LIFE as did the individual author. Neither was vitally concerned to distinguish between fact and fake; the saint was to be praised and extolled, and his LIFE was intended to instruct, convince and convert, come what may. Much of the LIFE had doubtless been in circulation in an oral form over a long period, and the saint had become a hero in the mind of the people, the one and only hero, for it is always difficult for them to accommodate two heroes, together and at once. He plays a part in every situation of importance, irrespective of differences of time and place. There is emphasis on the concrete and the definite. Certainty regarding location is important, and there must be an explanation for features, usual or unusual, such as the hill in Llanddewibrefi, explained as the land which rose under David's feet; the land on which he stood must be identified beyond doubt. Another characteristic in the life and mind of the people, found also in the LIFE, is lack of originality. We encounter the same features, the same motifs, the same miracles. Here are portrayed types rather than persons of flesh and blood, and rarely do we come across anything new or different; the story is invariably dreary, dull and predictable.

Nevertheless, it is possible to learn much from these LIVES about old customs, monastic life, education, folklore and mythology, agriculture, and other aspects of the life of society at an early stage. The author seldom reveals his sources, and even when he does, we cannot always be sure that he is telling the truth. However, it is possible for us sometimes to identify his sources, which from time to time seem to consist of chronicles, biographies, bruts, historical inscriptions and other written works, oral tradition, pictures, images, etc., and the relics of the past. The LIVES have been interpreted as religious romances, which is what they were in many ways. Nevertheless, it is important to remember that they also formed part of the liturgy of the church and its services. They became the main subject of the saints' feasts, and gradually displaced the scriptures and homilies in the lessons. From an early period it was the practice for the Latin sermon to concentrate on the saint on his feast-day. There were collections of homilies or lessons on the saints, suitable for delivery on their feast-days, but later in the thirteenth and fourteenth centuries the LIFE itself came to be read instead of the homily on such days, and even in the homily on the Sunday stories from the LIVES were used as illustrations.

The most interesting of these LIVES for us is that of David, at which we shall take a closer look, in both the Latin and Welsh versions. Professor Rice Rees, a predecessor of mine in the college I now have the honour to serve, as far back as 1836 described its contents as *the fabulous legends invented respecting him [David] . . . a mass of absurdity and profaneness . . . these wretched imaginations of a perverted mind.* Such 'a mass of absurdity' is the most illustrious example we have of this genre of religious prose. It was a composition with essentially practical and political aims, one of innumerable such documents to consist of 'wretched imaginations'. The 'perverted mind' was that of Rhigyfarch, one of the four gifted sons of Sulien, cleric, scholar and diplomat, who hailed from Llanbadarn and who was for two periods (1072–8, 1080–5) bishop of St David's. It was written towards the middle of the eighties of the eleventh century, in order to sustain the rights of the church of David against encroachment by Canterbury and the Normans. The church in the west, in centres such as Llanbadarn and St David's, had hitherto succeeded in preserving its independence; it was still non-diocesan, 'Celtic' and tribal in organization and outlook. Now, all this was being threatened, and leaders like Sulien and his son Rhigyfarch must have sensed the dangers that lay ahead. It was important that the founder of this church be recognized as one righteous and without equal, endowed with miraculous gifts, acclaimed as supreme by all in his own lifetime. In writing his LIFE, Rhigyfarch sought to display these qualities.

The angels had spoken of him some thirty years before he was born. An angel had come to his father Sant, king of Ceredigion, in a dream and foretold his birth. Next we are told how Patrick, who had hoped to settle in Vallis Rosina (St David's), was informed that he should move on to Ireland, as Vallis Rosina was reserved for one not yet born. David's mother was a nun, a virgin named Nonnita (Non), who was violated by Sant but who remained a virgin ever afterwards. His great powers are made manifest immediately after his conception. His mother never ate anything except bread and water; a preacher (named as Gildas in some manuscripts) failed to preach in her presence; miracles attended his birth and baptism. He was educated at Vetus Rubus, probably Hen Fynyw to the south of Aberaeron; then by Paulinus, possibly at Llanddeusant in northeast Carmarthenshire, where he restored the eyesight of his master. Having completed his education he travelled over large areas of south Wales and the midlands of England, founding churches in important centres such as Glastonbury, Bath, Crowland, Repton, Colva, Glascwm, Leominster, Raglan and Llangyfelach. He returned from his missionary travels, and eventually settled in Vallis Rosina, with three faithful disciples, namely Aidan, Eliud (or Teilo) and Ismael. There he had to contend with an Irish chieftain named Boia, whom he convincingly defeated. In his monastery there was emphasis on plain living, toil and prayer; stern asceticism and obedience were the order of the day, as his monastery was sought by kings and princes of the world, including Constantine, king of Cornwall. A series of wondrous deeds and events are recorded; springs appear and water is turned into wine. Aidan, David's disciple, with the sign of the Cross saved from the sea oxen which had fallen over the precipice, and a book he had left in the open air had remained dry, despite a downpour of rain. Subsequently, Aidan went to Ireland and settled in Ferns. On the night before Easter he was warned by an angel that poisoned food would be placed before David on the following day. Time was desperately short, but a disciple Scutinus was successfully despatched to St David's, to inform David of the plot. He arrived in time and duly warned the saint, but despite the warning, David ate some of the bread, with no ill effects.

Marvel follows marvel with unrelenting persistence, each one designed to underline the saint's pre-eminence. The cumulative effect is meant to be overwhelming, and to prepare the reader for two events which were to show beyond doubt that he was recognized as supreme by two authorities, the one autocratic, the other democratic. Accompanied by Teilo and Padarn, David went on a pilgrimage to Jerusalem, where they were welcomed with joy and honour, and where *the patriarch advanced David to the archbishopric*. Next we have reference to the great synod in Llanddewibrefi, a synod called in order to repel the heresy of Pelagius which, as we know, was prepared to recognize man's role in the process of salvation. All the country's kings and princes, bishops, abbots and priests came there. David was sent for and invited to come, although he had not originally intended to be present—one of the unmistakable indications of his modesty. However, he was ultimately prevailed upon to come, and succeeded in doing what others had failed to do, namely to preach so that all could hear. As a result, he was recognized by all as the greatest, was made archbishop of the entire British race, and his city was declared the metropolis of the whole country, *so that whosoever ruled it should be regarded as archbishop.* Finally, we are told of the consternation, when it became known that the end of his life was nigh, of the intense grief in Britain and Ireland. On the first day of March, *attended by the escort of angels, he sought the portals of heaven.*

Thus did Rhigyfarch seek to portray the life of David, to create a past that would serve the exigency of the present, and provide a propaganda weapon it was hoped would command the respect of people in high places. The language, of course, had to be Latin, the only language read and written over large parts of Europe. Some twenty-nine copies of this work have survived, among which we can identify five versions, one of them by Giraldus Cambrensis (c.1172–6). Early in the fourteenth century there was produced (possibly at Llanddewibrefi) a Welsh version. It is an abridgement of the Latin, and reflects spiritual and cultural vitality in Wales at this time, for which there is evidence from other sources also. It is one of many translations and adaptations of religious works produced during this period. In it there is emphasis on the simple virtues, on David's saintliness, godliness and wondrous gifts, but little evidence of concern with the weighty issues, which had affected Sulien and Rhigyfarch some two centuries earlier.

Not a single Welsh sermon has survived in manuscript. It was in the ninth century generally that attention was first given to the question of preaching in the vernacular. In his JOURNEY THROUGH WALES (1188) Giraldus Cambrensis refers to sermons by archbishop Baldwin, whom he accompanied, and also to an interpreter: *Alexander, Archdeacon of Bangor, acted as interpreter for the Welsh*. Over the centuries ignorance must often have presented a frustrating obstacle, for it is difficult to grasp how meagre and insecure was the clergy's knowledge of the Christian religion in the Dark Ages. There had been but little improvement by the second half of the thirteenth century, in the time of archbishop Peckham. We learn that parish priests did not preach every Sunday or Feast-day, and that giving instruction to their flock four times a year marked an improvement. And yet we have evidence that Grosseteste of Exeter had instructed his clergy to preach on Sundays, and had also given them some guidance on the content of their preaching. As for Welsh, the question to be asked is why so little homiletic material has been left, when there must have been at least some preaching in the language during the medieval period. Dafydd ap Gwilym refers to it in his dispute with the Grey Friar. If, as we are told, the Fifteen Signs before Domesday was often the subject of sermons from the pulpit in England, there is no reason to suppose that sermons on such subjects were not preached in Wales also. As we have already noted, the LIFE of a saint could serve as the subject of a sermon. Preaching must have become more common with the coming of the friars. This would doubtless involve the use of *exempla*, a collection of some twenty-four of which by Odo of Cheriton was translated into Welsh towards the end of the fourteenth century. This was done by a nameless cleric, probably from Glamorgan, at about the same time as a cleric from the same school by the name of Llywelyn Offeiriad produced in Welsh a version of the *Stories of the Seven Sages of Rome*.

Reference has already been made to the question of the extent to which the scriptures were known in medieval Wales. In his preface to William Salesbury's New Testament of 1567, Bishop Richard Davies of St David's expresses his view that Welsh translations of the Bible must have existed at one time, although he admits that he had never seen the Bible in Welsh. However, when a boy, he remembers seeing a translation of the Five Books of Moses in the house of an uncle of his who was a learned man: *pan oeddwn fachgen cof yw cenyf welet pump llyfr Moysen yn Gymraeg, o fewn tuy ewythyr ym 'oedd wr dyscedic*. It appears that what he actually saw was a copy (probably incomplete) of a widely known medieval text, with the Welsh title Y BIBYL YNGHYMRAEC *(The Bible in Welsh)*. This is not a version of the Bible, or of part of it, but rather of the *Promptuarium Bibliae (Key to the Bible)*, which is a synopsis of the historical books of the Bible, one of a series of prose and metrical synopses known as *Bibliae Pauperum (Bibles of the Poor)*, designed in the first place for the poor scholar or clerk. This Welsh version of which twenty copies and more are extant, is a rich repository of Biblical proper names and of Welsh versions of Biblical terms and phrases. It is not a mere translation of the *Promptuarium*, but contains some additions, in particular a complete translation of the first chapter of Genesis, of which there are two independent versions in the manuscripts. Y BIBYL YNGHYMRAEC was probably produced towards the end of the thirteenth century or the beginning of the fourteenth.

Another work, produced about the same time, in which there are scriptural passages, is GWASANAETH MEIR, the Office of the Virgin Mary, which has already been mentioned. One of the passages in it is the Annunciation *(Rybud Gabriel at Veir* Luke 1: 26–38), of which another independent version is found in the BOOK OF THE ANCHORITE. It was obviously thought that parts of scripture justified and required translation, especially those which were of use for the purposes of worship. Another passage considered to be important was *In Principio*, the first fourteen verses of St John's Gospel, of which translations occur in a number of manuscripts, including Peniarth MS 5 and the BOOK OF THE ANCHORITE. In a text called *Y Groglith* we have a translation of Matthew 26:1–28:7, which gives an account of the Trial and Crucifixion; there is also here an account of the finding of the Cross. Several copies are extant, including those in Peniarth MSS 14 and 5. Further, we can refer to translations of two other important passages, the Ten Commandments and the Lord's Prayer, as well as scattered verses in various texts, translations derived directly or indirectly from the Vulgate. Finally, there are a number of Biblical passages in *Y Seint Greal* (an adaptation of two independent French grail texts), found in Peniarth MS 11 (end of fourteenth century). Another version occurs in Mostyn MS 184 (end of fifteenth century), which we know to have been read by William Salesbury. Indeed, there is no lack of evidence that those who produced our Welsh Bible in the sixteenth century were familiar with these earlier translations.

In the early part of the sixteenth century, in Elis Gruffydd's Chronicle, which contains the text *Deuddeg Pwnc y Ffydd (The Twelve Subjects of the Faith)*, there occur translations of scattered verses, as well as some continuous passages, such as Ezekiel 37:1–13. A translation of parts of the Gospels, which brings us close to that of Bishop William Morgan, is found in Havod MS 22, a manuscript of the third quarter of the sixteenth century which contains some seven hundred pages of theological material, including the *Elucidarium* and *Kyssegyrlan Vuched*. The scriptural portions seem to be based on the Vulgate and on Tyndale's English translation. The name of the translator is not known, but he must have come from south Wales, as is shown by certain linguistic features. These passages were published by Professor Henry Lewis in Y CYMMRODOR 31 (1921), 205–13.

There is plenty of evidence in the sixteenth century that attention was given to the question of helping the parish priest to perform his duties adequately. Literature was provided to this end, most of it consisting of translations. There are extant some interesting manuscripts containing religious and other texts, such as the one in the possession of a priest Dafydd ap Griffith, written in 1515 and now known as Llanstephan MS 10. Another, which belongs to the early sixteenth century and which also contained a mixture of texts, was owned by Hugh Pennant, who translated the *Legenda Aurea* into Welsh. It is now Peniarth MS 182.

Reference has already been made to the *cwndidwyr* of Glamorgan. In the same province and at the same period we have evidence of the activity of prose translators, who were clearly concerned with providing instruction on moral and religious matters. There was a translation of part of John Mirk's LIBER FESTIALIS, consisting of some fourteen of the seventy-four homilies in the original work. A translation was produced also of the GESTA ROMANORUM, a collection of moral stories about saints which could be of use to preachers in their sermons. DIVES ET PAUPER was the name of a well-known work in dialogue form where we are taught, among other things, that a sermon is more important than the mass. It was published in 1493, and was one of the most popular of early printed books. Llywelyn Siôn, a poet and professional scribe of Llangewydd in Glamorgan (c.1540–1613), produced two copies of the Welsh translation. We are indebted to him also for preserving the text of Y DRYCH CRISTIANOGAWL (*The Christian Mirror*), probably the work of the north Walian, Robert Gwyn—part of which was published in 1583. It may be an original composition, but could be a translation or adaptation of some other unidentified work. It consists of a short guide to the Church's teaching on sin and justification, and on the sacraments, with copious selections and quotations from scripture and the Church Fathers. Its contents seem to have been intended by Catholics for distribution or for declamation as sermons in Wales during the last quarter of the sixteenth century. Finally, we may briefly mention Y MARCHOG CRWYDRAD, consisting of a Welsh version based on an English translation by William Goodyeare (1581) of LA VOYAGE DU CHEVALIER ERRANT (1557). It reminds one of Pilgrim's Progress and seeks to show man's weakness for vain pursuits.

We should proceed no further in this survey of our religious literature, which covers almost a thousand years, as we are here on the verge of important changes. We have reviewed the works of authors during this long period who were all adherents of the Roman Church, the only church in the West. It has been said that there is little in their work that could be described as original. That is quite true, but nevertheless, the thoughts, aspirations, hopes and fears expressed by the Welshman over this long melancholy period are his own, in that they were experienced by him in his own environment, and expressed by him in his own language. Moreover, from within the confines of his own life and land we find him venturing into other domains. He saw and described heaven and hell, the one with enthusiasm, the other with conviction. Now he was to experience radical changes, in which old prejudices, old convictions, old solutions and resolutions, old hopes were to be replaced by new ones, but certain essential features which had characterized his life and thought in the past were to continue. Political power had been taken from him, never to be restored; an abundance of wealth and leisure, to pursue the finer glories of art and culture, had never been within his grasp. But he had sought and found his God, for whom from the beginning he had nothing but praise, and had discovered a faith which provided for him and sustained him in the midst of misery and hardship, enabling him to spread his wings and rise above the wretchedness of this life to observe finer, more glorious lands. We are reminded here of the hymn of Thomas Williams Bethesda'r Fro in Glamorgan, who belonged to a later period (1761–1844):

> *Adenydd colomen pe cawn,*
> *Ehedwn a chrwydrwn ymhell;*
> *I gopa bryn Nebo mi awn,*
> *I olwg ardaloedd sydd well.*

> *(Were I to obtain the wings of a dove,*
> *I would fly and wander afar,*
> *To the summit of the mount of Nebo would I go,*
> *To within sight of better lands.)*

And later still, in our own century W. J. Gruffydd said of the Welshman and his literature:

Nid rhyfedd bod y Cymro yn ei lenyddiaeth ddiweddar wedi rhoi mwy o bwys ar grefydd nag ar ddim arall: dyma'r unig fyd y gallai ef, druan, ledu ei adenydd ynddo.

(It is no wonder that the Welshman in his recent literature has placed more emphasis on religion than on anything else: this was the only world in which he, poor man, could spread his wings.)

A Select Bibliography

Davies, R. T., 'Medieval Welsh Religious Poetry 1100–1450' (B.Litt. Thesis, University of Oxford, 1958).

Evans, J. G., THE POETRY IN THE RED BOOK OF HERGEST (Llanbedrog, 1911). *R.*

Foster, I. Ll., 'The Book of the Anchorite' (The Sir John Rhŷs Memorial Lecture, London, 1949).

Jones, G., A STUDY OF THREE WELSH RELIGIOUS PLAYS (The Bala Press, 1939).

Jones, O., Williams, E., Pughe, W. O., THE MYVYRIAN ARCHAIOLOGY OF WALES (Denbigh, 2nd edn., 1870).

Lewis, H., HEN GERDDI CREFYDDOL (Caerdydd, 1931). *HGCr.*

Lewis, H., Roberts, T., Williams, I., IOLO GOCH AC ERAILL (Caerdydd, adarg., 1972).

Morris-Jones, J., and Rhŷs, J., THE ELUCIDARIUM AND OTHER TEXTS FROM LLYVYR AGKYR LLANDEWIVREVI (Oxford, 1894).

Parry, T., GWAITH DAFYDD AP GWILYM (Caerdydd, 1952; arg. newydd, 1963).

—— A HISTORY OF WELSH LITERATURE, trans. H. I. Bell (Oxford, 1955, repr., 1962).

Williams, G., THE WELSH CHURCH FROM CONQUEST TO REFORMATION (Cardiff, 1962).

Williams, G. J., TRADDODIAD LLENYDDOL MORGANNWG (Caerdydd, 1948).

Williams, J. E. C., 'Medieval Welsh Religious Prose' (PROCEEDINGS OF THE INTERNATIONAL CONGRESS OF CELTIC STUDIES 1963, Cardiff, 1966. Pp. 65–97).

—— 'Rhyddiaith Grefyddol Cymraeg Canol' (Y TRADDODIAD RHYDDIAITH YN YR OESAU CANOL, gol. G. Bowen. Llandysul, 1974. Pp. 312–408).

—— 'Canu Crefyddol y Gogynfeirdd' (*Darlith Goffa* Henry Lewis, Abertawe, 1976).

The Author

Professor of Welsh and Deputy Principal at St David's University College, Lampeter, D. Simon Evans was born in Llanfynydd, Dyfed, and received his early education at Llanfynydd Primary School and Llandeilo Grammar School. He later studied at Swansea University College, the United Theological College, Aberystwyth and Jesus College, Oxford. He was lecturer in Welsh at Swansea University College between 1948 and 1956, when he became Professor of Welsh at University College, Dublin. In 1962 he was appointed lecturer in Welsh at St David's College, Lampeter, and later in 1966 became Head of the Department of Celtic Studies at the University of Liverpool. He returned to Lampeter as Professor of Welsh in 1974.

His studies are in the main concerned with the language and literature of the medieval period.

*This Edition
designed by Jeff Clements,
is set in Monotype Spectrum 12 Didot on 13 point
and printed on Basingwerk Parchment by
Qualitex Printing Limited, Cardiff*

It is limited to 1000 copies of which this is

Copy No. 0310

© THE UNIVERSITY OF WALES AND
THE WELSH ARTS COUNCIL, 1986

British Library Cataloguing in Publication Data

Evans, D. Simon
  Medieval religious literature.—(Writers of Wales, ISSN 0141–5050)
  1. Religious literature, Welsh—History and criticism
  I. Title II. Welsh Arts Council
  III. Series
  891.6'6'09382 PB2221
  ISBN 0-7083-0938-0